ESCAPE INTO THE
PSYCHIC KINGDOM

→ ESCAPE INTO THE
PSYCHIC KINGDOM

PATRICK MAHONY

THE INSTITUTE FOR THE STUDY OF MAN
Washington, D.C.

ISBN 0-941694-18-6

BOOKS BY PATRICK MAHONY

Out of the Silence
You Can Find a Way
Magic of Maeterlinck
Unsought Visitors
Barbed Wit and Malicious Humor
Breath of Scandal
It's Better in America
Who's There?
Escape Into the Psychic Kingdom

First Edition, 1964
First *Institute for the Study of Man* Edition, 1984

Copyright © 1984 by Institute for the Study of Man, Inc.
1133 13th Street, N.W., Suite Comm 2
Washington, D.C. 20005

To the Memory of my Mother

Mrs. E.C. Bliss

ABOUT THE AUTHOR

Patrick Mahony, the son of an Irish father and an English mother, was born in England, but educated in America. Growing up in California, the state which became his permanent home, his literary gifts led him to publish a large number of books in a variety of areas, ranging from humor and satire to travel and biography — but none were so popular as his books on the supernatural.

It is nice to know a lot — he argues — but if our beliefs and experiences were restricted to what can be explained, we would be but one tenth alive! Those who knew Patrick Mahony in life would surely confirm that beneath his urbane, assured, and courteous exterior, he fostered a deep interest in the possible survival of the human soul after death. But in his books he does not allow such convictions to take the edge off this ability to recount ghost stories with subtlety and humor. The result is a comfortable warm feeling about life — and even death — totally free from depressing fears about the world "beyond."

Most of the author's adult life was devoted to writing, lecturing, travelling, and to entertaining a wide circle of friends and acquaintances in his attractive home, nestled in a small canyon below the famous Hollywood sign which stands high in the hills above that exotic center of the imaginative and the bizarre. Conservative in his own life style, Patrick Mahony was nevertheless a talented host, and his well-known soirees attracted an ever-changing diorama of the famed and the talented. Those who were fortunate enough to be his guests will long remember his skills as a raconteur, for as Rene Fulöp-Miller expressed it: "I found that Mr. Mahony's stories held me enthralled in fascinated interest. The explanation lies in the fact that Mahony is a skilled reporter who knows a good story when he sees one, and refuses to spoil it for his readers by imposing upon them his own theoretical interpretation. I can only say that a weekend trip into Mahony's world, where three times three can be ten or eleven, is a wonderfully refreshing change from everyday life."

INTRODUCTION

When I interviewed George Bernard Shaw in the summer of 1946 at his Hertfordshire home, he was on the last lap of his earthly cycle. My first impression was that he looked more elegant than his photographs and possessed to a remarkable degree the air which is the sign of genius. Smiling benignly from the tufts of white whiskers which, together with his horn-rimmed spectacles, gave him an owl-like scowl, he cut through the opening commonplaces of our interview in the friendliest manner. "So you want to take a tour of Bernard Shaw. Have you ever taken a tour of yourself?"

Cocking his beard in an engaging manner, he proceeded to interview me! I quickly told him that all my life I had been fascinated by the subject of psychic phenomena, well aware that he took little stock in it. To his objections I quoted Einstein, who had once stated publicly that he believed it takes several illusions to make one reality. This sparked in Shaw an impish Irish mood.

"Years ago, when we were living in Adelphi Terrace, off the Strand," he said, fixing upon me his basilisk eyes, "Einstein and his wife came to dine with us. It was a full moon night in August and I took the old chap for a stroll along the Thames embankment. I casually asked him how far away the moon was. Of course, he had the answer on the tip of his tongue, whatever it was. I replied to him 'There you are quite wrong. Tonight the moon is obviously about a mile and a half away from us—because appearance is reality!' I was determined to show him that someone else could confound common sense besides himself!"

I did not see how this applied to psychic phenomena, but en route back to London on the train, I had an uncanny experience, known to many people who travel by that means. Another train went by in the opposite direction, and for a brief moment I felt the confusing sensation of going in the contrary direction to which I was supposed to be going. I only wished that this experience could have occurred on my way to see Shaw, then I could have used it to argue, as with psychic events, what we know to be happening, and what actually happens, are not always the same. I also got Shaw's point—that due to our system of educating people to rearrange reality, sometimes we do not see sensibly what we think we are looking at.

There was a time, not so long ago, when psychic phenomena had few proofs and, as a faith, only "faith" to offer. We have all vaguely known that we have a portion of the sixth sense but it was an unknown quantity, not backed up by other senses or research. Now, as an established science, it bids fair to help man wrest from nature a new concept of himself as well as the universe. It may explain ultimately how the finite and the infinite converge, and why the soul of man weighs absolutely nothing.

Perhaps the time will soon come when it will be discovered where the ganglia of cells, used by telepathy, is located. Now that the brain is being studied bio-chemically, we are living in times of great breakthroughs in this field. The Russian experimenters claim that they have been able to isolate and preserve psychic energy artificially. They have been successful in "photographing" the human aura—that normally invisible haze broadcast by all living things—by means of a microscopic lens and a special high-frequency generator.

The Russian Government has been spending millions of rubles on experimentation and development of all forms of psychic phenomena, while the Washington authorities are only now funding a few American institutions and organizations for this purpose—so we are not as far ahead as we might have been. Fortunately the period for denigration of this subject is over—that outrageous prejudice which held Sir William Crookes up to ridicule and kept Sir Oliver Lodge from his just award of the Nobel Prize for his stupendous contribution to Physics.

We who have pioneered so long, pleading for tolerance instead of scorn, are winning at long last. A cry has been swelling and increasing in volume from the general public, demanding understanding, as well as knowledge—hence still another book! New light, new knowledge, and new results from the Psychic World are yet to come, with the good and ill of all they involve.

Part of this book attempts to show how the inner life can be expanded. I offer few rules, if any. In fact I would rather my readers make their own deductions from the text. In my own case, I have found that understanding the psychic world has changed my life. Instead of being restricted to an ever narrowing path, it has unfolded for me an ever widening horizon. The ultimate aim of the book is a philosophic one.

It has also helped me to answer three important questions: Why am I here? What am I doing here? Where am I going? Therefore other parts of my book take an excursion into the immaterial, a world of thoughts and images, of the possible and the impossible. I feel that, without gleams of the supernatural, man cannot be completely assessed as man or Nature as Nature.

Those whom this part of the book may frighten, I can assure that no harm can come provided a positive mentality is maintained. However, if shut out entirely the good as well as the ill of the spirit world is kept at bay, which would be a pity. Whatever the soul discovers, the intellect must sacrifice, even if only a little.

I am indebted in many ways to many people. I believe it was my mother who first sparked my interest in this subject and not my Irish father, who was killed in the Great War when I was three. My mother was a beautiful but shy Englishwoman, who never thoroughly understood the harsh realities of the mundane world, so she took refuge in her dreams, some of which came true for her. I can remember her singing to me, when I was a child, in a pleasing amateur voice, the folk songs of faraway lands, which she called an expression of a country's soul. I noticed that she found in her private psychic world a perennial melody which gave her the happiness she did not find outwardly.

I am much indebted to the widow of my friend, René Fulop-Miller, for her gracious permission to use her husband's fictionized version of Count Koritski, which appeared originally in *Fortnight* Magazine. I am grateful to *Psychic* and *Beyond Reality* for permission to rework pieces on Stewart Edward White and Maurice Maeterlinck which I wrote for their magazines. As in my previous books on this subject, I have filled in the lacunae for certain stories which were told to me verbally and are, therefore, the memory of a memory.

Lastly, for me the act of writing has never been easy. This deep-delving into the mind is, I believe, an agony which varies from author to author; and in my declining years it becomes more painful! That is why I am not a prolific writer and why I only publish a book every few years. Critics have sometimes deeply wounded me, which makes me feel that few have complete awareness of the extent to their powers for good or ill. Do they know that they have no more avid readers than those they criticize—none more sensitive to what they think? To them I would consign the abstract message of this book, which is that we can far better understand the psychic universe by looking within than by peering into the dark corners of a haunted house.

CONTENTS

Introduction   v

Section One

The Inner Kingdom   1

Make Friends With Your Subconscious   5

Psychic Prophesy   10

Tremendous Trifles   22

The Magic of Serendipity   28

A Funereal Warning   36

An Etheric Poetess   37

Section Two

Retrocognition; The Future Within the Past   40

A Gift from the Grave   48

Music from the Dead   50

Telepathic Folklore   56

The Haunted Ether   59

Mechanisms of the Aura   62

The Buried Relic   67

Posthumous Painting   70

The Revenant Model   72

Section Three

E.S.P. and Plant Life   75

Animal Communication   80

Inspiration from Scenery   84

Intuitions of Emotions   89

Out of the Body   93

The Power to Will   97

A Phantom Companion   99

The Faces on the Cathedral Wall   101

Section Four

Our Eternity   103

The Light Beyond   109

Maeterlinck's Search for Phenomena   116

A Forgotten American Seeress   121

Lincoln's Dream   123

Esoteric Thirteen   125

Psychokinesis and the Evil Eye   129

Section Five

A Mystical Experience   133

Phantasms Across the Sea   143

The Irish Saint of Lunacy   146

Modern Exorcism   148

Two Cases of Somnabulism   150

A Message of Conspiracy   155

Lines to Live By   157

SECTION ONE

THE INNER KINGDOM

"Try to understand everyone else's inner life and, if they wish, let them understand yours!" cried Marcus Aurelius, the great Roman Emperor who preferred thought to power. He was referring to the thought-atmosphere every human being creates within the mind. This inward life of which Aurelius spoke, can be made today into an impregnable fortress from which we can face any assault. It can be the starlight of our lives. If it is sad, you can make it glad—just by changing the ambience.

Today most people are escaping from that which they pretend they are trying to find. They rush from one social gathering to another, divorcing themselves from the contemplation of innermost recesses of the soul until they end up spiritual invalids. Not that a certain amount of socializing isn't important to us. It quickens our wits and teaches us to mask our true selves, which cultivates self-control.

But going from party to party does not foster the happiness we covet. To know the joys of the inner kingdom, make up your mind you are not the average person—then see in your lot the best to be had. Tell yourself the best of tailors could not make a suit of clothes to fit you more perfectly than your own soul. Ignore the common hourly oscillation from the instinct of the ego to the lower depths. It happens to everyone.

Every inner life is perforce an interior struggle. Read the diaries of Thomas Moore or Walter Scott in which they

1

recorded conversations of thought with themselves, rebelling against the world of skillful egotisms and active ambitions—a world in which they were forced to deceive by smiles as much as by retorts they would have liked to make. They are examples of men who found life a compromise between what is known as commonsense and personal ideals.

Put mathematically every human situation constitutes an equilibrium of opposite forces; ours is a unique struggle working within the limits of our particular equilibrium. Unless trained to grapple with these opposing forces, how can the ego confront every day problems and keep you happy? First learn to know what you are, then you will understand what you are not. What better course, then, than to attempt to discover the principles that govern your life?

One way to liberate the inner life and use it for peaceful privacy, is to use the technique of the stage actor. The best actress or actor knows that acting, originally linked with religion, has a spiritual content. Become an actor for a few moments and picture yourself as a spectator. Scrutinize yourself socially and historically. Go miles down into your innermost being so you may see yourself as others see you—that outward self which Robert Burns yearned to know but never could. The result will surely astonish you and arouse your curiosity.

The great American naturalist, Henry David Thoreau, possessed this capacity of withdrawing from the outward into the inward to a marked degree. He is a superb example of a mental strongman and gave the world a model of a single human strength. He recognized that all our problems lie within ourselves and that every man's fate *is* himself. He came into collision with his times and decided to retreat within.

Thoreau won his battle of the inner world. His aim was not only to learn from the contemplation of Nature but to achieve independence from the outer world. Out of this experience came efforts to share his knowledge with others, and finally led to the publication of his immortal book *Walden,* which eventually made him wealthier than ever he wished to be. The book proves that he possessed rare forms of E.S.P.: he could catch a fleeting fish by thrusting his hand into the stream; he could guide himself through unknown forests at night; he could gauge any cubic contents, with utter accuracy, by sight.

Thoreau became, in a rather remote sense, an American Hamlet. No character could have been more self-distressed than Shakespeare's Hamlet. Yet he says: "I could be bounded by a nutshell and still count myself a king of infinite space," and this from a character who is a pure and noble man of fine moral stature, to whom all duties are obligatory—yet he finds himself inadequate to cope. Impossibilities are required of him and he sinks, but not completely. To the very end he was king of infinite space, in spite of the fact his mind held secrets of grief, uncertainties, even evil thoughts. All his woes and worries he kept from his consciousness by indulging in the reverie of a well-stocked mind.

So how do we stock our minds? Maurice Maeterlinck, perhaps more than any other writer, has stressed the value of the inner life. He felt we should store our waking mind with as many happy events as possible. We can do this, he said, by taking mental snapshots. This can be accomplished by a simple but workable psychic device. When you have an ecstatic experience—the one which makes you say "If only this could last forever!"—sanctify it in your memory, with all its fugitive subtleties, by picturing mentally yourself back at home—reflecting upon the event as in the past. Close your eyes as you make this reflection and see yourself remembering it back at home. Do this the same way that a camera lens opens and shuts—and the scene will remain etched in your memory-storehouse until needed. These outstanding memories should be tabulated and recited every once in a while, so that eventually they can accompany us as psychic luggage when we make the transition into death.

Another friend gave me a similar mental tool for the development of the memory-storehouse. She was a Polish woman who had been wrongly imprisoned by communists in Russia and placed for five years in solitary confinement. Thus she was thrown upon her own mental devices, with no reading material and no company. To keep her sanity under such untenable conditions, she began digging into her subconscious for events of the past. Mental walks she took, through places which had impressed her when traveling in happier times abroad—hardly believing the detail with which she could relive the joys of wandering through Rome, Venice, or Poland, where she had not been since girlhood.

Without anticipating solitary confinement, try this valuable exercise of memory regression—perhaps a walk of discovery taken years ago somewhere you loved. You will be astonished at the recondite events your mind will conjure up, and in so doing you will be using the quickest out-of-the-body experience known to human beings!

A man by the name of Xavier de Maistre (1763-1852) wrote a classic called *Voyage Around my Room,* after being detained in barracks while soldiering in Italy. He was allowed no books to read, only pen and paper. He employed his idleness to develop his inner world by describing a detailed account of his cell—the sparse furniture and even cobwebs on the walls. This exercise illumined his psychic powers and he was able to bring up memories of happier days.

Why not try this exercise the next time you are detained while waiting at a railway station or an airport for your connection? Besides watching the pageant of life, which is always instructive, take a mental voyage. Not only will you be insulated from the outer discord, but you will be benefiting from marvelous practice at withdrawing into the sanctuary of your inner consciousness, also communicating with the depths it contains.

You can use your inner ear to record mentally precious conversations with those you love—phonograph records which never wear out, never scratch, and cannot break! I have many of these records which I can listen to, and become refreshed, whenever I feel in need. With this device a life, gone physically from sight, cannot be lost.

As you learn to revel in the vaulted corridors of your inner life, a new consciousness will come to you. I can only say that this practice has brought me great benefit. In developing mine, I have learned to appreciate the changing shades of my own personality. I simply become a spectator of myself within, to witness the tragi-comedy of my own destiny. My inmost being has often been amazing. It unfailingly provides insight into the material world, over which it has important animating powers. Instead of living on the surface of things, I have possession of the place where the ultimate residence of self is. I apprehend myself, if not in my atomic makeup, at least so far as my spiritual equilibrium is concerned.

The inner life is a place of refuge, too, from the coarse ingratitude of others, the derelictions of friends, the ill-wishing of enemies. It cannot guarantee permanent happiness, because existence itself is clearly meant to be a struggle which must bring dissonance, but it does offer periods of perfect harmony, like calms between a storm. We would be miserable not to be miserable once in a while because unhappiness, now and then, is as essential as shadows to fine painting.

Outwardly you will still remain yourself. What use is it to wish to be someone else, anyway? Socrates made this point very forcibly when once asked if envy of others was wrong. He replied that if all our personal misfortunes were put into a common pile from which each of had to take an equal portion, most people would take their own and say no more! What you can expect from a new inner climate is a better resistance to unhappiness. To sum up, seek beauty and all else will be added unto you.

MAKE FRIENDS WITH YOUR SUBCONSCIOUS

Everyone has within himself an invaluable friend whom so few ever get to know. This friend has powers almost as inexhaustible as the Universe itself. Are you making full use of the tremendous resources available in your submerged mind known as the subconscious? Just because it lies buried deep in the primitive caverns of our mental jungle, it is disregarded by casual people. It lives on a totally different plane from the intellect, but is equal to every imaginable situation and, though it exists in another world, it is in close touch with our instincts—providing what is known as intuition.

Since the word unconscious is used for subconscious by learned psychiatrists, I shall use the latter word throughout, believing that the expression unconscious must mean zero of our consciousness—which is never the case. I might prefer the word subliminal, which was the nickname given the subconscious by F.W.H. Myers to connote the threshold of perception. But this has been adopted distortedly by the T.V. media.

I believe it was Sigmund Freud who claimed to have discovered the subconscious, but anyone who has read Dostoevski's novels will know that the great Russian has priority. Freud, however, discovered that it has no comprehension for the word No! It must be used mainly for wishing affirmatively. Needless to say, using it in this way one should not confuse it with the philosophy of prayer or, when using it against illness, medical advice must not be overlooked when needed. Prayer is reserved for spiritual support only, nothing materialistic.

Dr. Emile Coué (1857-1926), an obscure French pharmacist, became aware that our waking mind represents a very small part of our total psychic world. He helped millions to find its treasures through his system of autosuggestion which will forever bear his name. He also ran a series a clinics for the application of his remarkable theory. The basic premise was to dictate to your subconscious mind the slogan "Every day in every way, I am getting better and better!" He urged his patients to use this not only for illness but also to get more out of their lives. In so doing he was only beginning to utilize this power, and to find the real treasures is up to you. I can only tell you how they can become recognizable and give you the mental tools, as I am able to understand them. From this buried citadel we can only receive promptings and hints by understanding how to send in our requests.

Entering the contact with it should not be taken casually. It should be a vital experience and one which can be improved with assiduous practice. Always ask its help in a spirit of humility, wherever possible making requests that will help others beside yourself.

The process to be followed might be compared to planting a seed. You sow it in fertile soil, then leave it. The seed then unfolds according to the exact life-picture held in its ancestral cells. There the comparison ends because, in the brain of the weaver, the thought-picture must be clear and decided. It may be some time before the thought-picture is ready to present, so that it will have the proper meaning for the underlying consciousness.

Take care to paint the picture you wish to be realized, in your mind's eye so that it exists and stands out in all its perfection. Do not forget the minutest detail of the thought-form, then rehearse the words you feel describe it. Now you are ready to transmit it to that part of your mind which is capable of realizing it for you.

Do you wish to feel better? Surround yourself with an image of yourself representing all that health and well-being can offer. Picture yourself looking the way you wish to be, or picture the glow of your healthiest photograph. Do this just before going to sleep at night at the stage when the body is no longer believed to be you. It is then that all thoughts can be concentrated and the emotions are calm, when the oscillation of the intellectual processes cease and perfect poise can be assured. Then and then only, does the conscious begin close communication with the subconscious. When you want to feel better, do not say, as some New Thought religionists may recommend, "I am not ill." If you have an illness which seems to be only functional, and not serious enough for medical help, describe clearly what is wrong and ask to be rid of it. Besides thinking your plea in words, recite it out loud. Speak to your subconscious as if you were reciting a Mantra—that inspired ritualistic formula used by the Hindus for many centuries.

Or do you want more peace of mind? Then visualize

yourself looking serene with all about you *couleur de rose.* Say aloud, "Please help me find repose." And repose will come, you may be sure.

Do you need help with a forthcoming business deal or perchance a conference where the odds seem to be against you? Do not begin by saying "I shall beat my adversary," as any conceited fool would do. Before going to sleep on the night prior to the decisive meeting, intone words like "Please give me the quick wit and my best ability for tomorrow."

Then paint the thought-picture on the loom of your sleepy consciousness as emerging victorious and as if it were over.

These steps presuppose that you have taken practical moves to solve these problems and that you are asking help in situations which are not impossible to change in your favor. You must make only reasonable requests and you must have confidence that the seeds when planted will have the power to germinate within and without. This confidence will surely come after the first realization of your requests. Even if you have a few failures, these will be far outweighed by successes, as you will discover. The personal problems, ailments, or just plain annoyances which beset your waking life will be lessened until eventually you will look back upon a life you wished for. Cast your bread onto your subconscious mind and it will come back cake! And if the subconscious could speak it would say "Believe in me and I will reward you."

Never admit into your consciousness any thoughts but those about accomplishment in case any negativity might filter below. If you have defects, become aware of them and keep on putting them into reverse. Dwell always on the perfect qualities you admire in others and visualize them as your own. Enlisting the aid of your subconscious does not obviate the need for making conscious efforts, and the means of obtaining cherished results may only come in hints as you polarize your thoughts in silent meditation. Outward effort is an essential complement to what is done for you from within. As you cement this friendship, your intuitions will become keener and more unerring in their aid.

Someone has likened the technique for this training to

8

riding a bicycle. First you have to learn the secret of balance which usually comes in one mysterious spontaneous moment after several unsuccessful tries. However, I would liken it to learning riding on the back of a temperamental horse! As with the subconscious, you have to guard against being too firm and tense or the horse becomes unruly and uncooperative. Like the horse, the subconscious understands the sympathy of the experienced rider with whom it feels at home, even if the load is a heavy one!

The hunch is a strong, intuitive impression of what course to take and derives from the old superstition that good luck can come by just touching the hump of a hunchback! The word really means being sensitive to the conviction that we should take a certain action or not take it. In most personal or business problems there are several alternatives and the hunch projects·sometimes are the most difficult approach to the final solution. Oddly enough, it is seldom the one which logic would indicate and so often following our hunch leads to an amazing sequence of events. After maze-like turnings, we are guided to a fairly successful conclusion. We congratulate ourselves and seldom the subconscious mind, which is the true benefactor.

If this hunch came from your subconscious without any request by you, then you have received a bonus for which you have already been paid dividends! The majority of people will attribute hunches to the faculty of internal or second sight. Many people receive these hints and ignore them until the realization of one strong hunch brings them all into sensible relationship.

However, before you seriously start using your hunches, practice with those which come to you for unimportant matters or decisions. This will allow you to experiment to find out what proportion turn out in your favor. If the average is good, then you know you are making headway with your subconscious. Your best results will come when you can include others in utilizing your hunch and you must always want to deal with a situation, the solution of which is honorable. When anyone is motivated by a sense of honor, forces of good spring up to collaborate—even in these sad times when man-made justice so often seems to go to the wrong-doer.

Mention should be made about low psychism, such as cursing or illwishing, which is against all the canons of every religion. There is a real danger to one who enunciates a curse; it is done only at the expense of the soul. Enemies who injure you knowingly will receive their just deserts without any psychic ritual on your part.

I have seen many of my own enemies suffer without any wish on my part. When one of my closest friends, a Broadway producer, treated me treacherously and defrauded me of a production for a stage play of mine, I did serve him with a writ because he interfered with my contract in an illegal way. But I finally decided to leave him to Nemesis, a fate far worse than any curse I could have levied on him. As they say in Ireland, curses are like chickens—they come home to roost.

Using the subconscious for the proper purpose will soon teach you a very important part of yourself. Using the subconscious really works and the only limiting factor is if you allow your thought-atmosphere to be negative. So never think in negative or limiting terms. Just affirm constantly to yourself what you wish to happen and always conduct yourself as if you were already what you wish personally to be.

Think of your mind as an immense spiritual pyramid, the apex of which is your consciousness. The deepest segment of this pyramid is your subconsciousness. The deeper you can penetrate into it, the more you will find yourself at one with events of earthly and cosmic importance.

PSYCHIC PROPHESY

As we scan the screaming headlines of the daily newspapers we can rarely glimpse the inner lives of the people featured below the bold typeface. Why did this man, formerly wise and virtuous, fall into this fault or commit that crime? Why is a lady, said to be in full possession of her faculties, tempted to ruin her life in a scandal which tarnishes her name? Why does the private world of one seemingly innocent family fall into ruins while that of another glide along in blissful happiness, even though its members are obviously less skillful and wise?

Why does tenderness and love lie along the paths of some of our friends, while for others there is hatred, treachery, and malice? We see what appears to be only good fortune for one and for another nothing but continual collisions with misfortune. We see so many born with genius and all its rewards, while a majority suffer from disease, poverty, and stupidity. Does God run his own game of roulette?

The fact is very few people question fate. They tell themselves that what happened to others was bound to happen. Of course, they may wonder why a man, endowed with the fullest intelligence, would ruin his reputation by the commital of a felony; or why misfortune should befall the undeserving, especially when every precaution against it seemed to have been taken. They shrug their shoulders and do not ponder further.

Let us suppose we actually knew a victim of one of those fates and something of the mistakes made to cause the downfall, naturally we tell ourselves that in the other's place we would have handled the difficulties differently. We are vaguely aware that the spectres of accident, sickness, bankruptcy and even death, lurk around the corner but few of us, the very few, attribute the explanation to the agency of the supernatural or the preordained, where the answer most likely reposes.

A man known to the world as Cheiro, destined to go down in occult history as one of the finest of modern prophets, became haunted by these types of mystery in the days of his youth. Obsessed with the erratic vagaries of chance, he looked for a better explanation than the old bromide "What will be, will be." His real name was Count Louis Hamon, later to become world-famous under the pseudonym of

11

Cheiro (Greek for palm). He was born in County Meath, Ireland in 1862. I became acquainted with him and his wife when they came to California in 1928. Irish through and through, he was a man with disarming charm. In the early part of this century he had become very well known through stunningly accurate predictions he made for many statesmen, members of royalty, business tycoons, and just society dowagers. They all came to the studio in Bond Street, London, where he employed his gifts to help them.

It was in those early days when he became absorbed with a singular psychic mystery: Why do great catastrophes usually claim far fewer victims than they should, compared with the normal likelihood ascribed to the laws of probability?

Thus he began a careful study of disasters where many had perished—shipwrecks, tidal waves which swept inland carrying hundreds away, and fires which took a heavy toll of public buildings, also major trainwrecks. To his eager amazement he found in every such calamity he studied, there were always a significant number of people who were able fortuitously to avoid being present through trifling twists of fate. By all the logic of human affairs they ought to have perished, but were saved, and often by ridiculous and capricious circumstances.

Cheiro's tabulations showed that in average wrecks which resulted in lost life, the conveyance would be carrying far fewer passengers than it would on a similar day when no disaster was to take place. He found that other catastrophes, which might have ended with great loss of life, were lessened by providential conditions which kept many who planned to be present, safely at home. What was this mysterious unknown intervention which saved many lives, Cheiro wondered.

Delving deeper into the question, he found that in every instance of mass death there would always be a small percentage who actually felt a presentiment of coming danger and therefore changed their plans. A larger percentage who were saved were not so newsworthy but sometimes reported, would be thwarted at the last minute from embarkation.

They suspected nothing untoward, but events conspired to constrain them from sailing, or from being present at the site of an earthquake, or a fire that would have consumed them, or at the seaside resort where the tidal wave struck. The excuses that saved them would vary. They fell ill and could not travel; they had a family sorrow; or they had a sudden lapse of memory involving the time to depart, a love affair, or even a delay due to wrong directions. In short, some capricious excuse saved their lives!

A famous aircraft disaster is typical of this caprice. On June 18, 1942 the internationally known violinist Joseph Sziegeti, was seated in a plane at the old Washington, D.C. Airport awaiting take-off. He was due to play a concert that night in Kansas City. From his window he saw a beautiful woman, smartly dressed and alone, running to the gangplank. There was an urgent commotion with the boarding crew and in a moment one of them came to the violinist's seat.

"Sorry, Sir, he said nervously. "There is a lady here with a higher priority than yours. Please return to the waiting-room. We will make what arrangements we can for you on another airline."

Naturally Mr. Sziegeti was irked with the inconvenience at the time, but it was due to war regulations. Learning later that he had given up his seat to Carole Lombard, the moving picture star who was on a bond rally tour for the U.S. Government, he felt better. She had displeased him on the carrier, but he and the world were shocked later by a bulletin that the plane had crashed with a loss of all on board.

Cheiro had already died when this ghastly accident occurred but he had predicted it in 1933 when Miss Lombard came to see him for a reading. He also told her of a forthcoming love affair which would be a great event in her life, and this came true. But his wife, Countess Hamon, recorded in her Memoirs that after this interview Cheiro confessed he had seen a configuration in the lines of her left palm which could indicate for her an untimely and violent death.

"I see her dying like a heroine," he said. "I did not tell her, of course, but it may be that she will die in some accident while making her last film."

As the world would later learn she died, as she would have wished—in line of patriotic duty.

Cheiro's intriguing theory about fate extends to many other disasters which he investigated. The marine tragedy of the *S.S. Calvados* is a case in point. It sank in the Sea of Marmora in October, 1913, with a loss of all souls on board. Caught during a sudden squall in the great current which runs from the Black Sea to the Aegean, it foundered and went down while she was en route from Marseilles to various Turkish and Asiatic ports. It must be noted that these ports, at that time, were not well served by any other shipping lines, hence on normal runs, the *S.S. Calvados* was filled with passengers. On this particular sailing, however, its full complement of one hundred and seventy-five passengers was reduced to only one hundred and twenty.

Fifty persons who were booked to sail had, for varying personal reasons, changed their minds. Some fell ill; others gave excuses such as a death in the family, a financial crisis or the cancellation of a business conference. And, as in other wrecks investigated, there were the few who felt a presentiment and cancelled. In the case of all who were saved, it would seem that the forthcoming tragic event was known to their subconscious, which, taking alarm for their safety, manifested itself through devious means and accomplished their salvation. Unknowingly these people owed their lives to these warnings but none, or few, would give credit to their hidden, but little understood, friend.

What then, of the great majority who aren't, if unaccountably, saved who go blindly to their tryst with fate? Circumstances that claimed their lives, such as the storm that sunk the *Calvados,* have been slumbering in the future of the skies, and with them their fatal plans to embark on it, which they are destined to carry out. To Cheiro there was only one explanation. Those who perished must indeed have been less adroit in heeding the warnings of their subconscious minds, or they were lacking in the amount of rapport the others had with it. Of course, had all the passengers been perfectly in tune with their subconsciousness and had heeded its machinations—no matter how subtle—working to save them, the *Calvados* would have sailed empty of passengers! (The law of averages would prevent this happening).

This and other investigations confirmed Cheiro's suspicions that the future of human beings is buried in the subconscious, where are known important events before they come to pass. It knows our future but we cannot remember it. So the clairvoyant, possessing a psycho-chemical power in greater abundance than most of us, is enabled to get en rapport with it and then "remember" flashes of it for us. Thus a very small minority who receive their own flashes go through life as favorites of the gods.

Those who punctually keep their appointment with bad luck, obviously belong to another category. We all know them in our coteries of acquaintances. They fall in love with the wrong person or suffer disloyalty of friends and partners; in fact they can be counted upon to pursue only those who will drag them down. They hire unreliable employees, or they invest in the wrong stock or bond. They are especially prone to accidents which could easily have been avoided. These are the people whom, we feel, should see signs of oncoming untoward events along the course of their lives like billboards, but they do not.

Patiently, Cheiro watched the workings of destiny in the lives of his clients and became more and more convinced that it was directed by the subconscious mind. To understand the subconscious likes and dislikes, then, would better explain why destiny persecutes some and favors others. Without such an explanation destiny runs its own Monte Carlo!

The answer to this profound riddle, after diligent researching, was that we can coerce cooperation from the subconscious. It can be coaxed to overcome its apparent apathy and then it will allow to filter through hints of upcoming dangers and prospective favorable opportunities. It was clear to him that many are burdened at birth with certain weaknesses and deficiencies which the subconscious mind is able to help, if tapped.

In his renowned book on Palmistry, Cheiro studied the charts from the hands of all kinds of people. He went to asylums, prisons, hospitals—even morgues—taking palm impressions. Through his success with the elite of society, he obtained photos of palms belonging to many famous persons. Citing Revelations "I will leave my mark on the forehead and the palm," he used the palm rather than the furrows on the brow which is the more ancient form of reading the future. The palm for him was the best focal point with which to get in touch with, and draw knowledge from, the threshold of the subconscious mind of a client.

Some clairvoyants use tea leaves, others crystal balls, but it is always a device to help contact the "subliminal," miles down in this submerged part of the human mind which "knows" secrets that, if divulged, can be of inestimable use to us. In correlating his study of palmistry with life histories he came to believe that many an influence which had mastered a person unfavorably, were often the result of a misunderstood fragment of subconscious mechanisms.

To become proficient in making world predictions, Cheiro went to Egypt where he studied the Pyramids. There he was to absorb the esoteric teachings of the early sages, the wisdom enshrined within the monuments. Everyone knows that whoever built the Great Pyramid must have possessed almost superhuman knowledge of the celestial bodies. It also exhibits in all its detail the most minute mathematical accuracy in regard to astronomical laws.

Quite some time before the celebrated English Egyptologist, Sir Flinders Petrie, announced his findings, Cheiro deciphered some of the hieroglyphics left there by the master occultists, and he came to the conclusion that the Pyramids were not memorials to dead rulers, as is commonly believed, but to the spiritual pilgrimage of mankind.

He discovered that in worshipping the mysterious powers within the sunbeams, the ancient Egyptians had also learned much of Astronomy and Astrology, thus discovering recondite knowledge connecting inspiration and scientific enlightenment. By following the motion of the sun, they had penetrated the mystery called the *Precession of the Equinoxes.* Moreover, he found evidence that the vernal equinox took place at the Great Pyramid on the occasion when the star, Draconis (now extinct), shone directly above it in 2150 B.C., on which date he based his timing for farflung future events.

Correlating these discoveries with other esoteric information he was able to accumulate, Cheiro worked out a series of predictions for future historic events. These he consigned to his book *Fate in the Making.*

"Predicting world events," he once said to me, "can be likened to the predictive aspect of Thermodynamics, that science which allows its adherents to forecast the changing conditions of the Earth's physical system by observation of its basic laws. As with psychical predictions, the method will not accommodate for the rapidity with which some physical changes take place. It is the same with clairvoyance. The time element is sometimes very far off. It is always hard to pinpoint.

"The true clairvoyant must possess genuine gifts denied to the average person. When I use my powers, I have to raise the cosmic vibrations of my mind to the point where it is no longer hampered by mundane matters. I must draw on all the psychic energy I can muster, thus increasing the sensitivity in my psychic centers. I can never "read" more than a few clients in a day. On certain occasions I am in a better clairvoyant state than others."

I asked him to make some random general world predictions. A smile came over his face, almost involuntarily. "I don't have to be clairvoyant to say that the future is somber. The cycle we are now in (this was 1929) has been coiling and recoiling for centuries. It is a cycle which will continue to be dominated by the two-fold motives of peace and prosperity versus contest and warfare. It should terminate when the equinoxes precede further, circa A.D. 2050. The Armageddon, the war to end all wars, will be triggered in the 1980's or before, and I would say, will be fought over oceanic rights of some kind or other—possibly fisheries. The resources of the oceans are to become more and more important.

The aftermath of the Armageddon, which will be won at appalling cost by the Allies, will be a series of benevolent dictatorships, especially for the United States. The situation here will become so acute that I see the decent faction of the population living behind barred doors, not daring to go out into the streets. The judicial system will have become so corrupt and inefficient, in dealing with crime, that no one will be safe from attack.

"How long this situation will last is hard for me to say, but I see the year 1976. as very important for America. The Bi-Centennial celebrations of that year will remind the world of all the good America has done and of the profoundly spiritual purpose for which she was born. I was a lad in Ireland during the Centennial celebrations of 1876 and the eyes of the world were on America. Apart from the mathematical reckoning of hundreds, there is the influential mystical and rhythmical element in them. Everyone's hopes for America in 1976 will, I fear, turn out to be forlorn.

"Psychologically fate times these centennial celebrations properly. In 1876 Americans had worked out of the disastrous financial panic of 1873 and trade was booming. That year was the first that American exports far exceeded imports. Edison had announced his incandescent lamp; the first sentence was spoken over Bell's telephone, resulting in the start of a new enormous industry for the world. The Centennial Exhibition at Philadelphia was leaving all visitors awed at America's greatness.

"I see a similar situation for 1976, during which a great political genius will be born in the U.S.A. who will eventually become President. This man will make himself responsible to God alone and the famous civil rights of America will be abolished for the public good. Through him, the Golden Age will begin and man will stop imitating his machines. Life will no longer be a game of dice, with everyone for himself. With thoughts as wide as the sky and as deep as the sea, this great President will obtain cooperation from all corners of the

18

earth. I see him dying prematurely, but not before he achieves world accord.

"Nations will now be grouped in their correct Zodiacal Affinities, ending unnatural frontiers. Races will understand and sympathize with each other. Men and women everywhere will draw from this a spirit of emulation as powerful as that now being furnished by the stimulant of selfish self-interest. The antithetical powers of good and evil will, of course, still exist, but mankind in general will act in a spirit of co-partnership as never before. This will be due to the new genius-President and what he accomplishes could last as long as a century after his birth."

Unlike most clairvoyants, Cheiro did not try to predict the end of the world because he did not believe in it. "For me, God is the greatest engineer," he told me. "He set in motion the immense clock which is the Universe. This clock is continually gathering energy and can never run down. In its psychic mechanism there can be no diminution or any deterioration. And so the human mind imitates it as being the archetype of immortality. Psychical research may yet provide aspirations and hopes even beyond the premise of personal survival."

A year to look forward to will be 1998, which represents the number of weeks in the life of Jesus. Since we base our calendar on His life, Cheiro was certain it would be vitally important for the Christian world. This would, he felt, be the year for the election of the President born in 1976, when he would be only twenty-two! Cheiro pointed out that William Pitt was Prime Minister of England at twenty-four. (This presupposes the current law for the age of Presidents will be changed.)

The first important Royal client came to see Cheiro in 1890 and gave him wide publicity. This was King Edward VII who held an intense interest in occultism. He was then Prince of Wales and came because he wondered why the numbers 6 and 9 had played such an important role in his life. Cheiro showed him, through his system of fadic numbers, that these sixes and nines were numbers governing his astrological signs, and that the months representing these numbers are April, May, October, and November.

Edward VII was born on November 9th. He married on September 6th. His sixth child was born April 6th and died next day. The Prince was crowned on August 9th, 1902. He died on May 6th, 1910, aged 69. Cheiro warned him that this would happen when the two important numbers joined.

I suppose Cheiro's best-known prediction concerned the Duke of Windsor. When still Prince of Wales, he came for a reading at the studio in Bond Street. Cheiro knew already his horoscope from previous study—the peculiar planetary conditions which caused the young Prince restlessness, a love of changing scenes. He had noticed the mercurial moods, in meetings on different occasions. The young man's relationships with women had always been a matter of speculation and gossip and, indeed, the palm lines put marriage at a late date in his life.

"Your affections are such that they pass from ardour to indifference very quickly," Cheiro told him. "Due to this fluctuation you will not settle down romantically until middle age. Then, I predict, you will marry a commoner, after a devastating love affair, and will voluntarily give up the right to be crowned King!"

What the Prince replied is not recorded, but Cheiro published the interview in his book of World Predictions in 1927 and the actual interview was several years earlier, which makes it all the more remarkable.

With increasing fame for his accurate forecasts, Cheiro was invited to visit Czar Nicholas II in Russia. In a daring London newspaper article, he had mentioned the unfavorable future he saw for the Czar and, apparently, His Majesty wanted to see if it could be averted. Cheiro was not surprised to be driven to the Summer Palace in a bomb-proof motor car. En route to the Palace, he saw the Royal yacht which he was told was constantly kept with steam up for emergency departure.

Face to face with the Czar of all the Russians, he was struck by the philosophic calm and the disarming charm of the ruler. "Your Majesty has little to fear for some years (this was in 1904). I see a world war commencing in 1914, but your life will be spared. However, I see great danger for your family and yourself in 1917. I suggest that, not later than the Spring of that year, it would be exceedingly advisable for you to move your family near a border of a friendly nation, if there is one. It might be better if you move out of Russia entirely at that time. Meanwhile, prepare for the fateful year of 1914."

The Czar thanked him warmly but insisted that the Russian people loved him deeply and would never harm him or his family. As for all the security precautions, such as the bomb-proof car, this was ordered by the Okrana, and so on. Cheiro asked permission to write of the interview and was given it gladly. An account appeared in the London *Sunday Dispatch*.

After the Russian Royal family was massacred by Communists on July 16, 1918, he wrote again for that paper which editorially pointed out he had been correct. Had the Czar followed his advice, he might still be living. Cheiro ended by saying, "Any power that tries to tame Russia now will find it wasted effort. She will eventually threaten the harmony of world order, but nothing will be done because nothing can be done, to stop them. The star of the new order will continue to rise whether we like it or not. The old order will suffer."

These few examples of predictions made by Cheiro can be multiplied many times by referring to his books, and they pose the important question: Are events, as foreseen by a clairvoyant, so absoluteley preordained that we are denied free will? The similar question of determination versus determinism has troubled religious thinkers for several centuries. The great Rabbi Ben Joseph Akiba, who lived during the first century A.D., propounded the paradox that prophesies may come true, but man still possesses free will. Contrariwise, Jonathan Edwards, the celebrated church leader of Colonial times in America, emphatically denied the concept of free will but exhorted his parishioners to fear heavenly punishment. One remembers, too, the argument of

Shakespeare, who referred to our fates being shaped by powers external to our wills.

Cheiro believed our futures are comparatively fixed, as the chart of the palm is etched at birth, and thus can only be altered by a minimum of personal predilection. The last time we met, shortly before his death in 1936, I asked him what he felt was the main usefulness of the clairvoyant. He replied: "When anyone has to choose between two probabilities, an experienced seer can use his innate ability to select the one for which the subconscious will present the least obstacles. A good clairvoyant can also fish up warnings, but my experience has taught me that few people heed them."

Thus it would seem that free-will plays little part in our lives, if Cheiro was correct, and that those for whom misfortune is slated have been caught up in a series of circumstances beyond their control. Mysterious powers have been influencing them for some time, urging them to take unfortunate steps. These steps must finally bring them to the site where grief is waiting.

Is this because they will not take note of omens put to them by the subconscious, or is it due to fate itself? "There is no such thing as chance, and what seems to us to be the merest accident springs from the deepest source of destiny," wrote Friedrich von Schiller. All the same, fate does provide loopholes, as we all know. I can only stress again and again that cultivation of the subconscious can make our futures more malleable.

TREMENDOUS TRIFLES

In our daily lives useful signs and symbols often pass unheeded. If observed and studied they may be used to trigger our conscious mind into making a right decision or taking the best likely course of action. Too often we miss opportunities in life because what we regard as little things can be sometimes the causes of big things. They can be the beginning, the point of departure, which can decide our whole futures! Find the right starting point and usually success will follow.

The ancient Greeks and Romans consulted oracles, which were places of inquiry where advice was thought to come from the gods. These were sanctuaries, such as those of Zeus and Dodono, where leaders went to ask pertinent questions. The answers were interpreted by special priests who were educated for that purpose.

In Old China, the *I Ching* oracle book was compiled in about 1140 B.C. and it is still in use. By means of geometric symbols and hexagrams, the seeker is guided to appropriate passages, divining them through the manipulation of yarrow plant sticks. The book has gone through many editions in the western world, for one of which Dr. Carl Jung, the famed Swiss psychologist, wrote a foreword. And in his autobiography, he told of finding a successful interplay of questions and answers by using the book. He stressed he would not try to explain how or why the book worked, but for him it did throw light upon his subconscious mind. Certainly one secret of using the *I Ching* book rewardingly is to have faith in its powers, or at least treat it with humility and sympathy.

Omens and oracles have been known to bring out the genius of highly gifted persons. My friend, the late Ruth St. Denis—that eternal flame of Terpsichore—told me of an experience with an omen which changed her dancing career and made her world-famous. It happened when she and her husband, Ted Shawn, were merely theatrical dancers. They were touring the U.S.A. with financial success but without the critical acclaim they sought.

One day, when they were appearing in a Mid-Western city, Miss Ruth's eyes were attracted to a drug store window where, in plain sight, was a cigarette advertising poster depicting the goddess of Isis smoking a Lucky Strike! To the imaginative mind of Ruth St. Denis, this represented more than just the goddess. She saw her future symbolized. After the contents of the poster registered with her subconsciousness, she made an exhaustive study of Oriental dancing, adapting it to a new form of expression.

One might say the future of wireless telegraphy was influenced by a newspaper comic drawing. When a boy, Guglielmo Marconi noticed a "funny" in the Sunday paper of his hometown, Bologna, Italy, where he was born in 1874. It was an artist's conception of Santa Claus being surprised by two Christmas bells, spaced above him at a distance apart, and each bell was "talking" to the other with Santa evoking surprise.

This fired the inventive imagination of the young Marconi who had been annoyed by a hand-bell his mother used for calling the servant to the third floor of the villa. Lethargically, she spent many hours in bed during the day, so the hand bell had to be rung loudly, and frequently, to reach the ears of the servant in the basement. The sensitive ears of the youth were offended by this erratic burst of sound, and he decided to take corrective action.

Already an electric prodigy, he rigged up a crude transmitter, made from an induction coil, battery, and oscillator, so that his mother need only strike a button to set off a signal which would cause a lever to strike a bell in the basement. Without realizing it at the time, Marconi was using for the first time in history a wireless signal with a specific message. A short time later, he publicly demonstrated his invention and achieved world fame.

Omens played roles in the lives of Bibical personalities as is recounted in the Old Testament. They were often responsible for momentous decisions for good or ill in olden days. Breasted's *Ancient Times* tells the story of Croesus, the wealthy Lydian ruler, who received an ominous message from the subconscious mind of a common fruiterer! Croesus was poised for attack, with his tented army, in 547 B.C., ready to go against the Persians.

On the very night before his planned onslaught he heard a fruiterer calling outside his tent—intoning that he had some special Caunus figs for sale. He sang the sales pitch in a somewhat incoherent way so that it sounded like the Latin for *Cave ne eas* (Beware of going). Immediately Croesus called together his military advisers, insisting that he had heard an omen. But they ridiculed him and he was persuaded to carry out the plans. In the battle next day, his army was routed and Croesus was deposed.

An omen was used by Micah when he was consulted in 875 B.C. by King Ahab, husband of Jezebel, asking about the advisability of attacking Ramoth-Giliad. Going into trance the last conscious sight that came to the eyes of Micah was a flock of sheep scattered on the hillside. He noticed that they were without a shepherd, which he interpreted as a negative sign. It is certain that he advised King Ahab not to attack, but the King's decisions had always been political and seldom had he ever heeded his oracles. He was mortally wounded the next day in the attack on the Syrian stronghold.

Lady Gregory, the celebrated Irish playwright and authoress of a book about Banshees, happens to be one of the few persons ever to be warned of her own death by the appearance of this particular type of omen. (The Banshee is a family ghoul which announces forthcoming death by its manifestation to a close relative.)

She was entertaining at her home, "Coole Castle," County Galway, and one of her guests was the famous poet, William Butler Yeats. All the others were ready for dinner, assembled in the library, when Mr. Yeats entered late and very agitated. Almost overcome with fear, he said, "I have just seen a frightening apparition with the face of nothing that could ever humanly exist or could ever die. A mass of hair, bright red, fell over her shoulders and her eyes—they will haunt me forever with their hellish gaze!"

Lady Gregory went white. "That happens to be a perfect description of my own family Banshee," she said sadly. "It means that someone I know very well in my circle is soon to die. . . ."

Within a week Lady Gregory was taken to a London hospital, where she died unexpectedly.

Yeats himself was one day to be the victim of a similar situation. Seven years later at Cap Martin in Southern France, where he was passing the winter with his wife, the great poet was recovering from a slight indisposition. He felt impelled to

25

take a walk one afternoon to a little church not far away from his hotel, planning to return in time for tea. He found the particular church and its pretty cemetery a good place for meditation.

Just as he arrived a soft rain began to patter. He walked straight up the path, bordered with moss-flecked graves, to take refuge inside the church. Reaching the door he was moved by some indefinable impulse to turn around. With no little amazement he saw seated on a low tabular tombstone close by, a lady with her back to him whom he had not noticed before. She was wearing a black velvet jacket with a narrow border of vivid white, her head of luxuriant jet-black hair being surmounted by a hat also of black velvet.

Actuated by a sudden desire to attract her attention and induce her to look towards him, he noisily opened the rusty latch of the huge door. Turning around to see the result, he was dismayed to find the lady had vanished. Undaunted he went to the seat where she had been but found no trace of the late presence of any human being.

The following day, on January 4th, he wrote to his friend, Lady Elizabeth Pelham: "I know for certain that my time will not be long." He was quick to recognize the Banshee warning and he closed his eyes forever on January 28th, 1939.

I once had a rather odd psychical experience on one of my trips to England, involving a vacant grave in a cemetery. I was passing a couple of days in the New Forest, Hampshire. One morning early I went for a walk in the surrounding countryside. Somehow I was drawn to a church, perhaps because it was small in size and by contrast had an enormous cemetery. The church was closed, so I wandered about the graves. Some of them were very old with quaint inscriptions. For some reason I could not explain, I was drawn to a corner of the churchyard where I found a large tombsite inscribed:

To the Memory of General Sir Ian Crofton
Of County Wicklow
1881-1959

I was interested to find a compatriot buried so far from

Ireland and I pondered how he came to be there, such a distance from home.

Next day I continued my train journey to Dorset, some eighty miles from where I was, to stay with some close friends. At a luncheon arranged in my honor next day, the first guest to arrive was a Lady Crofton. With a nasty shiver, I told her of my coincidental find that very morning. It was an embarrassing moment, and her voice quavered.

"That grave is my husband's, but he actually lies in Ireland. He died during the war while visiting his relatives there, and I intend one day to put his remains where he wanted them to be. I must really bestir myself as he hated Ireland and would not wish to linger on her soil."

Naturally enough I wondered if General Crofton was using me as a medium to nudge his widow to act and bring back his body to its rightful resting place.

Another experience I had on the same visit to England (1971), seemingly defies the laws of coincidence and proves how a trifle can have considerable significance. Before my mother died in 1968 in California, she was very anxious to contact a girlhood friend in London who had vanished with no trace. She was a Mrs. Heppel with whom my mother had been on the closest terms all her life and had been in touch with two years earlier. Letters sent to Mrs. Heppel at her London home were all returned *Unforwardable*. My mother even sent a friend to the address who was informed that Mrs. Heppel had left without leaving any instructions.

In London, I called on my mother's last remaining crony, a Mrs. White, who had also known Mrs. Heppel and was as puzzled as my mother about her present whereabouts. That she was not deceased, we were fairly certain because she was the widow of a prominent admiral and her obituary would have been published. Laughingly, Mrs. White said to me, "You are psychic, Patrick, why don't you 'divine' where she is?" I bowed out of such a chore because I had much else to do in my short visit.

In Los Angeles I had bought a British Railway pass, which allowed me to travel anywhere in Great Britain, and the very next day this pass was due to expire. To usefully employ it one last time, I opened my guide book at random and noticed that an old manor house was open for viewing on that particular day at Princes Risborough, in Buckinghamshire. I have always liked old manor houses and this one possessed an Adam staircase.

I took the earliest train to see this seventeenth century house and who should open the door but the son of Mrs. Heppel. He had just retired from the diplomatic service and he and his wife were the new curators of this house which belongs to the National Trust. His mother was still living but had become mentally ill. He saw no reason to pass on the painful news to her few remaining friends.

It will be seen omens move in an area of paradox, and it is by paradox that their truths can be divined. They are instruments which, we have noticed, can convert mental sensations into tangible ideas. The time may come when firm rules can be laid down for them. Meanwhile, reasoning from omens warrants only probable conclusions, yet in everyday affairs of life we must always act on similar assumptions, anyway. Even when the conclusion from omens seems to have been misleading, they can still guide inquiry and lead to discovery.

THE MAGIC OF SERENDIPITY

The device hidden in the word serendipity coined by Horace Walpole in 1754 and rediscovered in recent years, is really an extension of the Biblical scripture, "Seek and ye shall find." Looking for one thing often leads to the fortunate discovery of a greater. It is really an E.S.P. power which some have in greater abundance than others. When used to help others, seemingly it has better results. Who has not stumbled on an unexpected blessing when on a quixotic quest? The finest example that comes to mind is the chance discovery of America by Columbus when he was actually trying to find a new route to India. And next in importance would be the case of Alexander Graham Bell who, in trying to find an aid for deaf people, invented the telephone!

René Fulop-Miller, the renowned Hungarian-American biographer, wrote a fictional account of a Viennese character endowed with this power of serendipity. Using the name of Count Koritsky, he lived in cheap boarding houses, while helping his fellow inhabitants in surprising ways. By some psychic means, best known to himself, the Count was able to bring about introductions deviously for those in need of jobs. Much success always resulted for those he armed with his magic letters.

A modest, even timid man, the Count never took credit for his help. He was usually dressed in threadbare clothes, which hung drably about his old figure; in strange contrast his face bore no lines or wrinkles. Seemingly, he had what the mystics call "illumination," by reason of which he could see deeper into the human heart than those who judge by externals. Through his letters of introduction, boarders obtained jobs in civil service, newspapers, engineering plants, and elsewhere according to their talents. When thanking Count Koritsky, all he ever asked in return was summed up in one sentence, for which he became famous, "Help whoever you can without hesitation!"

Those who followed his request woke up, as from a dream, with love flooding their lives and filling their hearts. To everyone they helped, they passed on the magic formula, "Help whoever you can, without hesitation!"

The fame of Count Koritsky spread for his "open sesame" letters and he was plagued with requests from far and wide. Soon he found it necessary to disappear and his admirers put out a dragnet for his whereabouts. He was never found, and his identity papers turned out to be false. The police described him as the perfect "con man." In his trunk, left behind at the boarding house, was a piece of cardboard, topping some worthless belongings. In large capitals was written "Help whoever you can, without hesitation!"

An example where serendipity paid off handsomely was at Limoges, France, in 1755, when the local doctor was approached at his home by a tramp for a meal. Seeing the poor man's boots were very worn, he also gave him a pair of his own, which fitted him perfectly. Later, the doctor noticed the old boots left behind were covered with a sticky white clay underneath a coat of mud. He was an amateur student of botany and recognized an unusual type of soil which felt greasy to the fingers.

At that time, Limoges was the center for the manufacture of porcelain but the clay used was all imported from China at great expense and inconvenience. The doctor took the sample of the sticky material to a chemist who found it was very near to kaolin, the clay from China used in making the Limoges pottery. How the old tramp was located to ask where he had been walking to accumlate some of this precious stuff on his boots, no one knows, but found he was. The clay was traced to the mud-flats near an old Abbey at Saint-Yrieux, a few miles away. This discovery gave thousands employment throughout the years and made Limoges porcelain much more competitive with other wares.

Serendipity had a hand in the creation of another line of a celebrated chinaware. A little later on, the great English potter, Josiah Wedgwood, was traveling by horseback from Stafford, where he lived, to London. He observed that his horse was suffering from a severe inflammation in its eyes. Stopping at a stable he was informed that there happened to be an ostler at a nearby inn who had what was said to be a magic cure for this very condition. There Mr. Wedgwood proceeded and watched as this ostler burned a piece of flint to make a powder, then mixed it with water and bathed the animal's eyes. In a trice the affliction was gone!

Delighted, Mr. Wedgwood was even more impressed with the beautiful white powder made from the burnt flint. Later, back at his factory, he burnt some himself, mixing it with his potter's clay. After some experimentation, he found it formed a perfect suspension for certain other essential mineral ingredients. Ultimately it made possible the creation of his famous Portland vase, with all its translucent beauty.

Pity for the discomfort of a child led to the invention of

the pneumatic tire. John Boyd Dunlop (1840-1921) was an Irish veterinarian who lived at Belfast. His nine-year-old son had to bicycle each weekday to school over bumpy cobbled streets, and the child developed chronic backaches because, up until then, bicycles were equipped with solid rubber tires. Mr. Dunlop had never invented anything in his life before, but he suddenly thought of how he could help his son. One evening, after the lad returned home from his ride and in considerable pain, his father took a piece of hollow tubing, inflated it with the boy's football pump. Then he forced it into some canvas casing sewn together for this purpose. Lacing this round the wheels of the bike, here was the first pneumatic tire! It not only cured his son's physical woes and made Mr. Dunlop a fortune, but it also led to a vast improvement for everyone who rode automobiles.

Another great discovery which came through serendipity was the discovery by James Bradley (1603-1762) about the theory of spherical gravitation. The great English astronomer had been stymied for some time in his calculations over the complex phenomena in the behavior of certain stars. By chance one day a friend took him for a yachting trip up the Thames. He was not a good sailor and seldom went aboard a boat, so it would seem this trip was fated to be.

It happened to be a lovely June day and Mr. Bradley was seated on deck, relaxing. Gradually his eyes were attracted to the flag which was flying aloft the masthead. He found himself staring at it for many minutes until he noticed something rather odd. Every time the ship altered its course the flag flew in the opposite direction, even though the wind had not changed. Even more peculiar, he noticed that the flag was more affected by the rocking of the boat than by the wind.

In a flash of insight he realized that the relationship between the earth and the stars must be affected by the movement of the earth. Further study and analysis resulted in his world-shaking announcement about the abberation of light, an explanation which has been practically unchanged to this day. This discovery alone led to his appointment as

Astronomer Royal.

Serendipity can be credited with the *Star Spangled Banner* anthem of the United States. Its author, Francis Scott Key, was only an amateur poet and had never written any acclaimed verse before. He was the District Attorney of the District of Columbia in 1814, when he heard that a friend, Dr. William Beanes, had been illegally taken prisoner by the British aboard a warship anchored off Baltimore. Against all advice, Mr. Key went aboard the ship under a flag of truce and he himself was held on board overnight. The British were at the ready to bombard Fort McHenry.

From the deck of the British skip, Key marveled at the way his gallant compatriots were resisting; and Old Glory was still flying next morning! Thus inspired, he scribbled the lines which have become immortal, humming them to himself with an old drinking song *To Anacreon in Heaven.* He risked his life to save his friend and brought him and his family lasting distinction. Would he have done so had he not decided to rescue his friend?

By far the oddest instance of serendipic good luck was the discovery of the ancient Newgrange Tumulus in County Meath, Ireland, a cairn four thousand years old and unsurpassed anywhere in Europe. It was "discovered" by a cow in 1870! A local farmer noticed that the grass was greener on the mound where the tumulus entrance was hidden by centuries of overgrowth. One of his cows was ailing and he asked permission of the owner of the field to allow it to graze there. The animal benefited from the rich grass so much that it fell right through the underground tomb-chamber and had to be hoisted out by a crane.

And surely the most humorous of great serendipities was when Sir Alexander Fleming sneezed onto a culture-smear rather than infect a colleague with a cold—and discovered the bacterial enzyme which led him to develop the medical possibilities for penicillin. The mould had been known since 1881, but no one recognized its bactericidal powers. Sir Alexander found that the germs left by his sneeze were all dead next morning, and penicillin was born!

Every so often, additions to world knowledge are contributed by reseachers who set out to find a particular thing, but in the course of their work they were mysteriously urged to follow something else suggested by earlier results. These side issues have yielded better findings than expected by their original aims. One might cite the case of Sir Issac Newton. One day, at Woolsthorp Manor, his mind was reaching the pinnacles of thought when he was distracted by an apple falling from a tree in his orchard. This focused on the threshold of his subconscious and enlightened him on the laws of gravitation.

Doubtless many prehistoric discoveries were due to serendipic accidents. When the first of men cut his foot on a sharp stone, we can be sure he found a new method for skinning animals; or when he first noticed that plants grow from seeds, agriculture came about. Very much later, the first model for the pump was probably inspired by an animal's vivisected heart. Isn't it likely that connecting rods were imitated from human joints and bones? Hinges and socket-joints are copied from the human body. The miracle of the camera lens came from a study of the human eye. One could go on further, making one exception only—the principle of the wheel rotating on its axle, which man can claim as his very own original.

The symbology of serendipity is charmingly illustrated in an anecdote of Irish folklore. It is about an old farmer who, when dying, called round him his two prodigal sons. "Boys," he said, "before I leave you I want to tell you a great secret. A valuable treasure lies hidden on this demesne which you will both inherit." Then the old man's voice began failing as the sons asked in eager chorus: "Quick, Father. Where is the treasure hidden?" Choking for want of breath the Irishman answered: "You will have to dig for it!" And then he expired.

Forthwith the sons went to work with spade and shovel upon the neglected fields, but no sign of any treasure. So they decided they might as well sow the fields whose tillage they had unwittingly completed. In the autumn they discovered the treasure in the rich harvest of a bumper crop!

Nature is so wealthy, she will never run out of ideas. Since man was born she has been continually whispering to him, inciting him to partake of her ideas. We may yet learn through serendipity how to solve some of our pressing current problems. If the secret of nature's photosynthesis can be penetrated—how plants convert the sun's energy into living food—a new way of feeding suffering humanity may be evolved. Who knows?

* * * * * * * * *

As far as I am aware, there are very few serendipity ghost stories, that is to say about someone trying to contact one ghost and finding another more useful. Here is an example, told to me years ago by a Miss Anna Corney, a manicurist who used to visit my mother's London home when I was a child. She was a remarkable clairvoyant, although she allowed this only to be an avocation and she would never accept a fee, except for her manicuring. I remember my mother felt she was far better at fortune telling than attending the nails and cuticles. Certainly she had some remarkable credits for predictive accuracy.

She was a plain little lady, with penetrating eyes, obviously in close contact with the psychic world—so much so she would never accept an evening appointment for her work. She was too busy with her ghosts, who, she claimed she sought for help in her predictions.

There were, she told me, "regulars," who made frequent appearances and were presumably her guides. But one midnight she was in her small room in the so-called private hotel where she lived at Willisden Green, near London, when a young man dressed in military uniform appeared. He was a ghost she had never seen before but he did not come as any surprise to Miss Corney, as the year was 1917 and the war was raging; nor did it frighten her that the soldier had only one arm since such sights were common in those sad days.

He lost no time in explaining why he was there. "I want you to contact my wife who is non-psychic and you alone will be able to do this for me. She is very unbusinesslike and needs help urgently. Somehow it will be arranged for you to meet her." There followed a rather complicated financial transaction regarding some life insurance he had carried. He spoke the words exactingly, so that Miss Corney could remember every one of them.

She replied: "How can I contact your wife if I do not have her name and address?" But the words died on her lips and the spectral visitor vanished in the way they all do.

A few months later, she attended a new manicure appointment. It came from an advertisement in the local paper, and she had never met the lady at any time. When she arrived and had settled down to her job, her eyes drifted around the room because the lady did not seem to want to gossip as most clients did. With a shiver of recognition, she saw on the mantel-piece a photograph of the soldier who had appeared that midnight a short time ago. Nervously she dropped her nail file and cried, "Is that man your husband?"

The lady answered with a sob, saying that he was. "My husband was killed three months ago. I am mourning him deeply and so are my children."

"Then I have a message for you, Madame. He appeared to me some time ago and asked me to tell you something. . . ."

At first the client was adamant. "I do not believe in resurrection of the dead. Please change the subject. . . ."

Miss Corney persisted. "There is one way I can convince you, I believe. Didn't your husband have but one arm? Did he not lose it just before he died in the base hospital? You see I know what I am talking about."

The client's face went ashen white. "You must have been in touch with my husband. Please forgive me for doubting you." Then Miss Corney gave the advice which the man had asked to be relayed to his widow.

She was overjoyed. "That is exactly what he would have told me. You see I have been so puzzled over his insurance papers and now I can handle matters the wisest way. How can I thank you enough?"

A FUNEREAL WARNING

Over the little town of Ballinrobe in County Mayo, the Irish sun had been blazing all day in August 1893, but with the approach of midnight came a refreshing breeze. The Marquess of Dufferin was holidaying from his post as Ambassador to Paris and staying at the home of a friend. He could not sleep, so oppressive was the heat, and he got up to stand on the balcony of his bedroom for a few minutes.

A full moon illumined the sweeping greensward down to the brook which rushed swollen and foam-flecked beneath the garden bank, filling the night with strange eerie noises which suggested choked human voices, now rising into angry threatenings, now dying away in sobbing murmurings.

As Lord Dufferin's gaze sped through the shadowed country beyond, it was quickly brought back to the greensward where now he could plainly see a man walking with automatic steps and wheeling in front of him a barrow across which lay something large and oblong. When the figure came within closer scrutiny, the marquess felt a shudder as he realized that the thing on the barrow was a human-size coffin. The man was young and had a long, thin face with a straight nose, such as was characteristic of the native Irish workmen. And as he went wheeling on, he pushed the barrow from the grass onto the gravel drive, making a gritty sound.

Next morning Lord Dufferin naturally asked his host about the strange scene, inquiring if there were any funerals to take place in the district. But although all the ground employees were questioned, no satisfactory explanation could be found. No one would have any reason to transport anything at that hour, let alone a coffin. So Lord Dufferin agreed reluctantly that he must have had an hallucination, and in a few days he was back at his post, and the affair had gone from his busy mind.

Two months later the marquess was attending with his wife a formal reception in Paris at the Continental Hotel. A steward ushered them to the elevator, at that time a modern innovation, but as they were about to enter, Lord Dufferin clutched his wife's arm in a gesture of refusal. He gave some excuse—the car being too crowded—but what actually deterred him was the extraordinary resemblance of the operator to the man whom he had seen wheeling the coffin up the greensward of his friend's estate at Ballinrobe. The sudden shock gave him an ominous feeling.

As the elevator began moving upward, Lord and Lady Dufferin heard the sound of straining cables; then came a reverberating crash simultaneous with the sound of muffled screams . . . When it was possible to extricate the passengers it was found that all were alive though some of them seriously injured. Only the operator had been killed.

Naturally the premonition of Lord Dufferin attracted attention and the newspapers of the day featured the story. Inquiry about the elevator man was not without its curious side. The authorities found that his papers were missing and his references so obscure that his identity was never established.

AN ETHERIC POETESS

The theory that poetical genius bloweth where it listeth really is untrue. It is the poet who can make more publicity noise today who receives attention. These "mod" writers of verse rarely, if ever, attempt anything like a plot. You are always as wise after you read their poems as when you began. Never can you grasp what they are trying to say; probably neither can they. They speak of stars, sun, and moonbeams— but these were intended to shed light. With our successful modern poets what that something is you will never find out!

What a blessing it was when two American ladies, Mrs. Grant Hutchins and Mrs. John Curran, went to a downtown department store in St. Louis one August afternoon in 1923 and purchased a Ouija Board. Both were of average education and typical housewives, so imagine their excitement that evening when the pointer began spelling out pure poetry. It began: "Many moons ago I lived. Again I come. Patience

Worth my name."

Mrs. Curran seized the board nervously into her own hands and the indicator began rushing about so rapidly that her eyes had difficulty keeping up with it. "Wait! I would speak to thee. If thou shalt live, then so shall I!"

At that point, Mr. Curran, then employed as a civil servant in the Department of Immigration, entered the room. He burst out laughing when told what was happening. His wife held the board more firmly as the apex continued its hasty tracing, versifying the hurt feelings of the spirit:

> Am I a broken lyre
> Who at the master's touch
> Respondeth with a twinkle and a whir?
> Or am I string in full
> And at his touch
> Give forth a full chord?

There followed a brief biography of the spirit's life on earth. She was born in 1650, the daughter of a Dorsetshire weaver in England and an only child. "My thumb is thick from twisting flax," she added and spoke of delivering fine linen to castle folk. After her mother died she had been brought to America as an indentured servant and lived at Martha's Vineyard, near where she was later killed by Indians and "a tree grows out of my grave." (Investigations have verified that a woman by the name of Patience Worth actually lived in New England in the Seventeenth Century.)

By means of Mrs. Curran's Ouija Board, Patience continued to dictate poetry, also prose compositions, of literary quality. These were in a language which exhibited all the peculiarities of her period—about which Mrs. Curran could not possibly have known. This dictation spanned several years and Mrs. Curran, complete with her Ouija, took to the lecture circuit where she demonstrated spontaneously what Patience Worth could do. Poems of great philosophical worth flowed from this prolific mind in the ether, as for example:

> Who would pray, let him then
> Make his prayer the sheath of the sword
> And not the sword. Let him then

Make his prayer the goblet to contain the wine
Yet not the wine. Let him then
Make his prayer a casket of alabaster
In which to keep the jewel, not the jewel.

Enough superior verse was collected for a book to be published, which sold exceedingly well. Francis Hackett, renowned for his literary criticism, pronounced the work to be of great quality, "sensitive, witty, and keenly metaphysical." Another critic classed Patience Worth with Emily Dickinson and Elizabeth Barrett Browning—so after such extravagant praise there was naturally a reaction. For a few years interest in her poetry was very little. (In 1930, however, just after Mrs. Curran died, a revival was manifested and something like a fair estimate was made.)

The controversy angered Patience, who told Mrs. Curran, "I am a weaver of cloth and the cloth I measure is not for him that hath. Thou shalt take a wee one and thou shalt deliver the goods of me into its hands.

So Mr. and Mrs. Curran, directed from the Beyond, sought a female baby to adopt. The one chosen turned out to have the red hair and blue eyes Patience said were hers on earth (this child could still be living). Meanwhile, Patience composed books to pay for the child's upbringing. *Hope Trueblood,* a novel about pirate life, became a best-seller in the 1920s. The New York Times commented: "Whoever Patience Worth is, she measures up as a fine writer."

The last book to come from this spirit guide, before Mrs. Curran joined her, was *A Sorry Tale,* a story of the life and times of Christ. It was eulogistically praised by Professor Roland Greene Usher, Dean of History of Washington University, who pronounced it to be "the greatest story of Christ penned since the Gospels were finished." He pointed out that if Mrs. Curran had not been a woman of fine integrity she would have claimed the distinction of authorship for herself. He said that it would be well-nigh impossible for a scholar to write continuously in seventeenth-century English without committing some minor anachronisms, which never occurred in the writing of Patience Worth.

SECTION TWO

RETROCOGNITION; THE FUTURE WITHIN THE PAST

A friend said to me recently, "If only I could come face to face again with those dear souls who have been my all in all and who have disappeared from this earth. Would I not give a year of my life just to have them with me even briefly. There is so much I would like to explain, so many kindly acts I neglected when they were living."

In how many minds does memory march waving this banner of regret? Yet there is a place where briefly we can commune again with those no longer of our dimension. In our nightly dreams we sometimes meet with them; here they are even more lovable than when they were in our midst. All that we disliked in them is unnoticeable, for they show no signs of those small pieces of temperament which we criticized. In truth they become the persons we always wished them to be.

Such dreams as these are activities of the soul and will be familiar to every sensitive reader. I would like, therefore, to explore instances where important intelligence has been communicated in the dream state—where images have been transmitted on a secret wavelength which somehow violently stimulates the psyche of the recipient. In these strange manifestations, comparatively rare, all the conditions which normally govern the sensory processes are violated.

Numerous playwrights, scientists, poets, and inventors have readily admitted their debts to dream sources. Professor Louis Agassiz (1807-1873), the renowned Swiss zoologist, was shown spontaneously in a dream how to piece together the bones of an extinct marine mammal which had puzzled him in waking life. In sleep he was able to see the correct skeletal arrangement for the mixed-up bones he had found during his excavations in Brazil.

Another scientist, Dr. Friedrich Kekule of Germany, discovered the structural formula for Benzene during a day-dream. Benzene is a colorless volatile liquid (not to be confused with Benzine), used for the production of a large number of organic compounds, and was formerly distilled from fish-oil in small quantities. Dr. Kekule was living in London in 1865, working at a laboratory there, trying to figure out the formula. All his colleagues had given up the quest, but not Dr. Kekule. One day on his way home on the top of a horse-drawn bus, the soft summer air had a somnolent affect on him. He dozed off for forty winks and, on the horizon of his semi-conscious mind, suddenly there appeared a vision of the traditional Chinese dragon.

The frightening creature formed a hexagon, with six distinct sides, quite different from the traditional serpent. It awoke the inventor with a start and the flash from the psyche of his subconscious mind enlightened him. He could now see that the benzene molecule is symmetrical and that the carbon atoms must be arranged in a hexagon. There must be one carbon atom in each of the six corners, with one hydrogen atom attached to each carbon atom.

Next day he went to work and invented a now-famous Benzene Ring or Hexagon, which revolutionized that particular part of chemistry. He gave credit to his dream atop the bus, for which some of his colleagues held him up to ridicule. He snapped back by quoting Sir William Herschel, the German astronomer, who said, "I have direct evidence of an intelligence working within me which is distinct from my own personality but which directs my train of thought into a channel it would not have taken on its own."

A similar fasinating dream incident comes from Dr. H.V. Hilprecht (1895-1925) a Harvard Professor who was considered an expert on quartz. He was stymied over two pieces of agate fragments which he found in Babylonia during excavations in 1913. He could identify them as belonging to the Cassite period (circa 1700 B.C.) but because they bore what appeared to be a disconnected sentence in cuneiform writing, he was puzzled how to interpret them in a book he was preparing. It seemed to him the pieces were part of a finger ring from a Babylonian male. He writes:

"About midnight, weary and exhausted by my attempts to decipher the inscription, I went to bed and was soon deep in sleep in which I had a remarkable dream. A tall, thin, priest of the pre-Christian Nippur period, appeared before me. He was about forty years old, clad in a simple abba gown and at once beckoned me to follow him. We entered a treasure chamber belonging to a temple and I found myself in a small low-ceilinged room without windows. In the middle was a wooden chest, and scraps of agate and lapis-lazuli were scattered on the floor. Then the priest spoke in a language which I understood although it may not have been familiar, 'The fragments which mystify you actually belong together but they are not from a finger-ring. Here is their correct history: One of our kings sent to this temple, among other treasures, some pieces of agate and lapis lazuli. One of these was an inscribed votive cylinder of agate. An order came to make a pair of earrings for a statue to a god—the god of Ninib. So we cut the agate cylinder into three pieces. That is why the inscription you seek to complete is impossible. You will never find the third part and neither can I!' "

Dr. Hilprecht did some further researching and, to his delight, found that the information from his slumberland priest really answered the riddle of the agate fragments. The inscription was impossible to complete but the first and third part suggested a tribute to the god of Ninib.

Premonitory dreams are more likely to be warnings portending unhappy events rather than joyful ones. John

42

Millington Synge, the great Irish playwright, went to the Aran Islands in 1898 at the suggestion of William Butler Yeats, who felt he might obtain material for some plays. The result was excellent—*The Well of the Saints, Riders to the Sea,* and *The Playboy of the Western World.* All blazing masterpieces of the theater! Mr. Synge found that much dialogue came from just meeting the denizens and listening to them speak. He was also aided by obtaining a room in a farmhouse where, through a chink in the floor, he could listen to the gossiping in the kitchen below. This provided first-rate dialogue for his plays.

When Mr. Synge first experienced what he later called "the dancing dream" it was on his visit to the Aran Islands. They are off the Coast of County Galway and their most remarkable feature is the quantity of early and pre-Christian ruins. He was staying at Inishmaan where the high cliff faces have a barren, supernatural beauty.

The night before he was scheduled to depart after his long stay, he experienced this weird dream which he wrongly attributed to a psychic memory of the past. It was clearly a warning of his approaching illness, one which was to linger with him for the next ten years and finally killed him because he did not heed the warning. He was dead at 38 from lymphatic tuberculosis.

"Last night," he wrote in his book on the Aran Islands, "after walking in my dream among local ruins lit by an intense light upon them, I heard a faint rhythm of music far away, played on a stringed instrument—possibly a harp. It came closer and closer, gradually increasing in quickness and volume with an irresistibly definite progression of import-ance. When it came very near the sounds began to move within my nerves, even my blood, and to urge me to dance. I knew that if I yielded I might be carried away to some moment of terrible agony, so I struggled with myself to remain quiet, even holding my knees with my hands.

"The music increased continually, loudly tuned to some forgotten scale and a resonance as searching as the strings on a cello. The luring excitement of its power became more and more evident, greater than my own will, and my limbs began moving in spite of me. I was, in fact, swept away in a whirlwind of musical notes. My breath, my thoughts, and every impulse in my body became a form of dance until I could no longer distinguish between the instruments and the rhythm of my own consciousness.

"For a while it seemed an excitement filled with joy; then it grew into an ecstasy where all existence was lost in a vortex of movement. Somehow I could not believe there had ever been a life for me beyond the whirling of this dance, until the ecstasy changed into a rage of agony. In my struggle to free myself it seemed that the passion of the steps increased. I shrieked in protest, but the voice could only echo the notes of the music.

"At last with a moment of uncontrollable frenzy, I awoke. I dragged myself to the window and looked out. The moon was glittering across the sea, but there was no sound anywhere."

According to his fiancé, Maire O'Neill, who starred in several of Synge's plays at the Abbey Theater and elsewhere, he had this dream periodically during the next ten years. She was with him when he died in a Dublin hospital on March 24, 1909. Not long before he recognized it at last as the allegorical representation of the Dance of Death. Had he heeded it earlier he might have guarded his health more zealously and perhaps lived to realize his full artistic stature.

As regards the strange dream music, Miss O'Neill told me, Synge one day heard it played by a fiddler on O'Connell Street. He discovered it was a ballad composed by Turlogh O'Carolan (1670-1738), the blind minstrel and last of the Irish bards, who wandered through Ireland with his harp. Was it possible that he wandered to Inishmaan as a ghost?

It seems many artistic people have premonitory dreams. Perhaps it is their ability to record them that makes this seem so. Samuel Taylor Coleridge's early work shows little trace of the powers which were to make him famous until, one night, he had a dream in which he heard himself composing a poem which he knew was perfection. In acknowledgement he called

44

it *Vision in a Dream* and later it was rechristened *Kubla Kahn*.

Among dramatists for the legitimate theater, the case of William Archer (1865-1924) is a very interesting one. He was the author of a great box-office success called *The Green Goddess*. Before this he was only a well-known theater critic for a leading London daily, and author of an important book on playwriting in which he baldly stated that he did not feel he could ever write a successful play. He was as well a practicing spiritualist and member of a circle formed by Sir Oliver Lodge, the famed physicist whose researches into electrical science helped to bring radio to perfection.

Soon after the end of World War One in 1918, Mr. Archer was staying with some friends in Cornwall, in the district known as the Lizard. The house was an ancient mansion, reputedly haunted. On the second night of his stay there, he had a dream in which his eyes became fixed on the seated image of an evil looking six-armed goddess colored green. "It was placed at the entrance of a huge, primitive type of palace," he wrote, "built with long stretches of rugged masonry and crowned by Oriental turreted arcades."

Suddenly there was the reverberation of a crash and next he saw a group of white people extricating themselves from the wreckage of an airplane. They were wearing aviation helmets and leather coats and, to his amazement, they were being watched by a group of rudely clad natives, Mongolian in feature. They were chattering among themselves, while a man of higher stature and more Aryan in looks, seemed to hold authority over them. He was clothed in gorgeous temple costume and robes.

Then, led by a procession that comes down a mountain path, an Indian raja enters the scene, headed by a Negro flourishing two naked sabers. He is followed by a dozen musicians, then by a litter carried by four bearers. Inside the litter is the Raja dressed in fantastic attire. His servants help him out and he proceeded to dictate the story for the play to the dreamer.

Perhaps the most curious aspect of dreamland is the way

the mental processes seem to be at once the cinematographic projector of the scenario as well as the audience. In our dreams we appear to be two different personalities. We may watch our own funeral, as did Abraham Lincoln in the famous dream he recorded just before his real assassination. In the land of dreams, the subconscious mind invests itself with nothing less than the supernatural so that it can carry us into lands we have never visited and where all obstacles are overcome with the greatest of ease. It was this universal experience of primitive man with his dreams which rooted his mind so deeply in the supernatural.

Dream prophesy is yet another argument for the hypothesis that the subconscious knows the future. It wisely screens out many of the unpleasant events in store for us, or our waking life would be filled with fears and worry more than it is. There is an exceptionally engrossing example of an anticipative dream which was responsible for convicting some dangerous criminals.

Judge Matthew Doherty tried a case of murder in the High Court of Dublin in the early part of this century. At the finish, he instructed the jury in what he felt was a *prima-facie* case of homicide and he felt gratified when a verdict of guilty was voted. He donned the black cap and passed sentence of death upon the defendant, who uttered a curse but was otherwise unmoved. The case had produced some grisly evidence in which the murderer, who was a hired assassin, had dismembered the body of his victim in order to dispose of it.

Judge Doherty had decided, before the unpleasantness came to an end, that he would need a change in the countryside to forget it. So that he could catch a late afternoon train, he had his handgrip all packed. He had taken such trips alone before, temporarily forsaking his family, forgetting those responsibilities, and just reveling in a visit to somewhere he had never been before.

This time he decided to visit a village named Ferns, County Wexford, once a stronghold of the Leinster kings. He took the train to Gorey, a nearby town where he would find a hotel, in order to take the further trip to Ferns on foot next morning. It was late evening when he arrived at Gorey and he put up at the first inn he came across. It was called *The Jeanne d'Arc,* and he was amused to recall another of the same name he had once seen in France which advertised an English grill!

This inn was far from elegant, although many years earlier it must have been a hostelry of distinction. The ornate wrought-iron porch was well preserved and over the doorway were elaborate effigies depicting Joan's ordeal by fire. He was quickly brought back to the present when he was met face to face by the innkeeper's wife. She resembled a character out of the French Revolution, such as one of the *tricoteurs,* who knitted while the heads were rolling from the guillotine in 1792. This ugly woman showed him to his room where its dilapidation disturbed him even more, but he was too tired to seek another shelter. In Ireland, country hotels are usually far from fancy.

After the woman left, he was further perturbed to discover a ladder at the windowsill going down to the ground two stories below. As a precaution, immediately he placed the dresser in front of the window to prevent any possible intrusion. Then, dismissing any more anxiety, he went off to sleep.

What could be more natural than for him to dream of the innkeeper himself, whom he had never seen. The man appeared at the top of the ladder in this dream, entered the room with knife in hand, and then stabbed the Judge to death! Very vividly he saw all this occur. Then he watched the man unlock the door and let in the evil-looking wife. Together they carried the prostrate body of the Judge downstairs and in the omniscient vision dreams provide, he followed them as they carried his body into an outer building. There the nightmare ended. The Judge, sleepless from then onwards, paid his bill as early as possible next morning, and left the inn.

About five years later, Judge Doherty heard of a murder at the *Jeanne d'Arc* Inn. Remembering every detail of his dream, he lost no time in journeying to Gorey, where he was

47

informed the preliminary investigation was in progress at police headquarters. Sure enough, there was the same innkeeper's wife and about to be questioned. She looked even more offensive and depraved than before. In her testimony she insisted the murdered man had been accompanied by a friend who had committed the crime, left the body in the stable, and then had disappeared. In those days no guest registers were kept at small hotels, so there were no records to disprove her statement.

Almost as if possessed, Judge Doherty, who was well-known to the local authorities, broke in brusquely, shouting, "What about the ladder perched at the windowsill? You know perfectly well that your husband climbed it, entered the room through the window and murdered the occupant. Then, together you robbed him and took the body into the stable. . . ."

Flabbergasted, the woman's face became contorted with surprise and rage. At first she screamed denial then, almost derisively, she cried back, "How comes it you know all this?"

Next, the innkeeper was brought in who Judge Doherty recognized as the man in his nightmare. He was seen by the Judge for the first time in person and had been kept waiting in another room. He had not heard the loud exchange of words, and the presiding magistrate informed him of his wife's reaction to the Judge's accusation. Thinking she had confessed to the crime, he made a move to throttle her. Later the two admitted their guilt. Their heinous crime had been enacted exactly as seen by the Judge in his dream.

A GIFT FROM THE GRAVE

The name of Mrs. Patrick Campbell is still apt to arouse varying emotions and reminiscences in those that knew her in person or remember having seen her on the stage. To her intimate friends she was a lovable woman whose very faults could but add to her fascination. At times, it is true, she was mean and vindictive, and especially towards the end of her career she would often fall back on inflicting petty humiliations on those around her. The treatment she meted out to many who tried to help her inspired the witty remark of Alexander Woollcott that she was "a sinking ship firing on her rescuers."

Some years before she died she fell seriously ill in her London home and was befriended by Sara Allgood, the sister of Maire O'Neill and who became later a feature player in the films of Hollywood. "I see myself already in the tomb," Mrs. Campbell said when she thought her life was ebbing. "I had hoped to get far away from here to die, to a place where I would not be known. There is a certain charm in being forgotten after a life spent before the public."

But the great actress rallied. She, who for years had filled the theatrical world with admiration for the power of her genius and fear of the biting sarcasm of her wry wit, now went to France, sad and broken-hearted and with but one thought: to die in peace. Before leaving she expressed her gratitude to Miss Allgood by giving her a few personal mementos, a teapot and a framed water color of a heron.

Not long afterwards Sara Allgood was called to Hollywood to make a moving picture, the result of which was a long-term contract. She bought herself a home, and the teapot Mrs. Campbell had given her was soon in use and the picture of the heron adorned a wall in her boudoir.

Being Irish, Sara Allgood believed that the first dream one has in a new home comes true. The peculiar thing about this particular dream was that every detail of it had the same exaggerated clearness as is characteristic of stereoscopic vision. On the horizon there appeared, as though by magic, a locomotive which whistled by at full speed. Everything was in its logical place as in a real view, but the absolutely distinctive feature was the emotion aroused when the train came to an abrupt halt some distance after it had passed the station. Mrs. Campbell alighted and came running up to her old friend. She was looking pale and wan, as though she had been undergoing a great strain.

Before Sara could express her astonishment, Mrs. Campbell

held a hushed finger to her lips. "Have you found my gift from the grave? Look behind the picture." These words were uttered with that sublime air of boredom which had been one of her admired feats on the stage.

The dream came as a surprise to Sara Allgood, for although she knew that her friend was then at Pau in Southern France, living there under Nazi occupation, a report had come through that Mrs. Campbell was safe and well. Next morning Miss Allgood immediately went to the wall and took down the picture of the heron, and removing the backboard, she found a caricature of the actress done by Max Beerbohm and signed by him. It was a gift worth something in excess of a thousand dollars.

In the evening papers a release from Pau announced that Mrs. Campbell had died in the previous night.

MUSIC FROM THE DEAD

Is it possible that a composer's work is sometimes impinged upon his mind by others already dead? Certain composers have admitted that a few pieces came much more effortlessly than others. Some of the greatest creators among the immortals suffered from unstable nervous systems, which could mean that the spirits may have found them the easier to use as mediums. Is there perhaps an infinite reservoir of music in the spheres?

Serge Rachmaninoff's masterpiece, *The Isle of the Dead,* is only one of several musical works inspired by a painting of a cemetery by Arnold Bocklin (1827-1901), where centuries ago the Neapolitans buried their dead in the Gulf of Naples—under the awesome shadow of Mount Vesuvius. His tone poem is a macabre piece and conductors usually prefer one of his many other works, so it is little played. The great Russian composer wrote of how he felt urged to write it.

First he studied Bocklin's painting for hours on end at the museum where it hangs. In an interview, he told of hearing voices from the dead while he was working on the music.

"Over the horizon, after sundown, they all came, all the voices at once—humming the music to me. Into my mind it came, surging. I synthesized it and wrote it down between April and May, 1907."

He was not the only one to set the ghoulish Bocklin painting to music. It inspired a musical fantasy by Heinrich Schultz-Beuthen. Its instrumental possibilities were exploited by the German genius, Max Reger, in his *Four Tone Suite*. Among others who felt the painting's haunting vibrations was Anders Hallen, who wrote a symphonic work, and Eugene Zador, the great Hungarian-American composer, who lives in Los Angeles and wrote an entire Opera he called *Die Insel der Toten*—using the cemetery itself as the scenery in the last act. This was performed at the Royal Opera House, Budapest, in 1928.

The music written for this painting suggests that composers received it from the spirit world. One feels it is music from another sphere, similar to that achieved by Richard Strauss in his *Death and Transfiguration*. In this, Strauss was inspired to translate into music the anguish of a dying man, his struggle with the spectre of death, and his psychic deliverance into the Beyond.

Gustav Mahler's music was always aloft and accenting the theme of the birth into glory. I remember a conversation with his widow long after he had died and she was married to Franz Werfel, the Austrian novelist. I asked her how Mahler was able to come so close to the mutation we call death and keep his music of our world. Her reply elucidates the clashing sonorities in some of his symphonies. She replied, "My husband was trying to get beyond music, the way Beethoven had tried." The latter, had of course succeeded with his sublime use of the pause. Mahler's music is always stressing the death instinct of man.

"You must remember," she went on, "Gustav had the power to see with his ears and hear with his eyes. He opened both to nature. For hours I have seen him gaze at a mountain lake, with its enlightening serenity. He insisted that there is no part of nature which does not contain a form of music. He would write music about fossils in an ancient rock formation, twisted with the petrification of centuries, and out of this would come interesting symphonic ideas."

One day he said to his wife, when she asked him why his music must always be so sad: "How can it be otherwise in a world where human beings whom you love have to die? I see death as the secret of life! It is the underlying idea of all my symphonies."

Music from the dead has brought into the limelight a middle-aged suburban London widow named Rosemary Brown, who is now obtaining a great deal of it from spirits of composers, notably Beethoven and Franz Liszt. When a child she had visions of the latter, and he told her he would come one day and dictate music. Little did she realize that she would become a musical medium for him and others.

Mrs. Brown grew up, married and had children. She did not give much thought in later life to her childhood visions, as she had seen other ghosts, as had her mother. Her knowledge of music was very rudimentary. She had never mastered the thirty-two bar pattern of the piano, but she continued to take lessons from time to time. However, she was not encouraged to continue by her teacher, who simply felt she was not gifted.

After being widowed, she obtained a clerical job to support her children. One night, upon her return from working, she decided to relax by strumming at the keyboard, as she sometimes did. The piano had not been tuned for years and had been in her home since she and her husband bought it—a typical middle-class house in the district of Balham. She had forgotten much of the music she had been taught and relied on her innate musical powers.

Suddenly, she looked down at her fingers, but they were no longer *her* fingers. She knew from the feel that she had no more power over them and they were being controlled by an outside force. So was her mind! She found herself playing quite professionally the work of a composer she had never heard before!

Then there appeared in front of her, without any sound

and as large as life, the looming figure of Franz Liszt, looking the same as had his ghost as seen when she was much younger. He explained, in a language she could understand with difficulty, that he had just "dictated" a new composition, and that he planned to give her others. Moreover, he promised to introduce her to colleagues, such as Schubert, Bach and Beethoven, who were waiting to use her as a medium.

She was frank with Franz Liszt. She told him she was a very poor musician and felt incompetent, but he replied that had she possessed expert musicianship he would be unable to use her! He said that she had been chosen from many other psychics because she was not well-trained but possessed perfect pitch, which would make things go the way they wished. And so the posthumous collaboration began.

At first Mrs. Brown was afraid to tell her friends about her work, fearful that she might end up in an asylum! Liszt kept his word by introducing her to several neighbors of his in the beyond, who appeared and dictated music to her. Laboriously, Mrs. Brown took down note by note what they gave her, always in their own particular idiom. Beethoven obliged with a bagatelle which experts on him say is better than any he composed while here on earth. It has been acclaimed by Richard Rodney Bennett and Humphrey Searle, the famed English composers.

Somehow a distinguished English educationist, Sir George Trevelyan, heard of her spooky work and persuaded her to show him some of it. He was much impressed by what he saw and encouraged her to tell the world about her séances. Thus Mrs. Brown came to the public attention and her activities were scrutinized by the fierce light of fame.

Opinions have varied about the quality of the work she receives. For the last two years she has been taking dictation from Beethoven for his Tenth Symphony, a choral work. While on earth he only had time to write nine. Mrs. Brown says that he is able to turn out much calmer music now because his hearing has returned. Meanwhile, controversy rages over the head of the little Balham housewife. It has become like a lightning conductor—so many storms have broken over it! She has been violently attacked and eulogistically praised. She takes no credit herself for the musical productions and insists she is only gifted with mediumship, which she inherited from both her father and mother. No one doubts her sincerity. Many who have examined her feel the music is coming from the original sources and that it would be impossible to fake it.

Another case where music was obtained from the dead reads like a detective story. It was told by the late Herman Darewski, who wrote such successful tunes as *K-K-K-Katie, Where Do Flies Go in the Winter Time?* and *When We've Wound Up the Watch on the Rhine,* as well as many musical scores for films and shows. Before his death in 1945 he was touring South Africa in a series of concerts. In one of these stops he was taken to see a place named Laing's Nek, once a noted landmark in the war between the British and the Boers, but now an isolated historical tourist attraction.

Just as the party was inspecting the old battleground, one of those typical torrential rainstorms began. Herman sighted an old farmhouse in the distance. They all rushed to it for shelter, and, like everything else in the district, it was deserted. Someone climbed through a window, opening the bolted door from inside. There they found an amazing scene of neglect. Cobwebs fought with the grime of ages. What little furniture left behind was in a state of disarray.

It took Herman to spy, hiding in a far corner of the living room, an old upright piano with candlesticks of brass. Immediately, soaked though he was, he settled down on a broken chair and began exercising the touch which distinguished him as a first-rate pianist. As he harmonized, more to cheer up his friends than anything else, he found his fingers picking out keys which blended into an exquisite melody, despite the poor tone of the rusty strings.

Everyone present was charmed by it and asked the name of the composer. Darewski was forced to say he did not know, because even he had not heard it before and it had not come out of his head. In fact, he added, he liked it so well he would take down the bars for future reference. As he continued to play, the rain increased so the party was forced to pass the night in great discomfort. The tune then left his mind.

Eight months later in Capetown, he and a friend attended an outdoor concert given by the Capetown Military Band. The two became bored with the customary pieces being played. They were about to leave when the band struck up the melody he had unwittingly played that night in the abandoned farmouse. It was the same piece, note for note. He was staggered. Afterwards he went to the bandmaster and asked excitedly: "Please tell me the name of that melody you have just played." And he hummed a few bars.

The bandmaster took him aside. "It's rather a strange story," he began. And the tale he unfolded was indeed weird. In the early part of the Century, there had been a competition for amateur band composers and this piece had been received. It was the only one of any merit out of hundreds submitted. The odd thing was that the man who submitted it, explained that he had not written it, which complicated the performing rights.

It seemed that the actual composer had been killed in the Battle of Laing's Nek in 1881. The man who made the submission had bought the old farmhouse inside of which the manuscript was found. He sent it in as a forlorn chance, for he did not understand music at all.

Since the music was outstanding, the bandmaster traced the relatives of the dead farmer for copyright purposes. They gave their permission and whenever it had been concertised, it was received with much acclaim. The mystery was to fathom why the composer had not written anything else that could be traced. How he was able to create such a lovely tune without being famous was anyone's guess. He must have been schooled in musical notation, but his relatives vouched that he was not really musical. All they would say was he never married, was very eccentric, and stated he would come back to haunt the old farm after he died. Naturally Darewski asked himself if he could have received the music from the same source as did he?

TELEPATHIC FOLKLORE

At one time scholars believed the great folk tales, such as *Jack and the Beanstalk,* originated in India and were diffused by traders, travelers and crusaders, since they were found in Greece and Russia. But when it was discovered similar stories were told to children of the Mongolians in Asia, the Red Indians of America, and the Zulus in Africa, long before the white man entered those lands, the theory had to be abandoned. The only explanation is in telepathy. These stories were mentally "radioed" throughout the world!

Irish literature would be greatly impoverished without its superb folklore. Its vitality is closely connected with social conditions because the Irish are a tribal people and, in reading the accounts of the heroes, they believe they are reading about their own ancestors. Many of the stories in this fine literature certainly began as true experience, but passed on and on, finally crossed the border into the imaginary. In the good old bygone days, the Irish storyteller had high social rank and narrated with great dramatic effect. Adults as well as children possessed the marvelous gift of escaping into the world of the imagination and the incredible.

Here is a typical yarn: a young man gets possession of a magic ring. The ring is stolen by his enemy, then recovered by a mouse he has befriended. The enemy who had stolen the ring hid it within his mouth, but the grateful mouse insinuated his tail into the nose of the thief, made him sneeze—and out came the magic ring!

This story is found in the Punjab, amongst the Bretons, the ancient Greeks, the Russians, and in Zululand. No one can tell with certainty the genesis of the authentic folk-tale. Sometimes they illumine the mystery of the human paradox or, as Freud pointed out, they can show deep insight into physiological truths which have been verified by scientific discoveries.

In Ireland there are still to be found these pieces of psychic flotsam and jetsam, beating feebly against the rising tide of materialism, and refusing to die. Here are two stories from different parts of the country which I collected during my travels. They are obviously attempts by early natives to explain some of the phenomena of Nature or the everlasting flux of human values. They may even inculcate morality or show that virtue pays in the long run, while vice goes to the wall. The stories are set in a period of pre-History.

The king and queen of the Blasket Isles are worried because they have no son and heir and the kingdom will expire with their deaths. One day they are on the beach and the queen feels compelled to take a swim. She strips off her clothes and wades into a crystal-clear sea. Gliding out to sea about fifty yards, she suddenly noticed, pacing her six feet underneath, a naked man. Frightened and shocked, she retraces her strokes back to the beach, where she falls fainting into her husband's arms.

In due course she becomes pregnant and the royal couple are overjoyed. A son is born who grows to manhood with one extraordinary trait—he never needs sleep! Otherwise he is strong, handsome, and a credit to them despite his nightly restlessness.

One summer evening a tramp calls and asks for hospitality, which the ancient Brehon laws require to be given without demur. He is lodged in the son's bedroom and, of course, notices that the young man is continually awake. "Do you never go to sleep?" asks the tramp.

"No," replied the prince. "I have never needed one wink of sleep in my entire life!"

"Then I know who you are," the tramp whispered in confidence. "You are one of the sea-people. That is why you never need sleep."

The prince goes to his mother next day and says: "Can it be I am one of the sea-people? Is that why I never need sleep?"

"Yes," the queen answers sadly. "I have always meant to tell you. Your father lives in the sea."

The young man then goes to the seaside, takes off his clothes, and wades into the water. When his body was nearly engulfed, a huge hand arises and embraces him, taking him under the rippling water.

Numberless are the stories about enchanted swans (attributed with remarkable powers), talking horses, grateful bulls, even magic frogs. One tells about the Irishman who feels he must go to Connemara before he dies, that part of Galway which is all sea and bog and sky and, to some, still the land of heart's desire. He goes into his mud cabin, starts packing his things, and his friends come to say goodbye. Connemara is nearly one hundred miles from Dublin and it was a major undertaking to get there on foot in those faraway days, so there had to be a formal leave-taking.

"Where are you going, Paddy?" they asked.

"I'm going to Connemara, where else?" the man replies.

"You mean you're going to Connemara, God-willing!"

"NO!" answers Paddy, emphatically. I'm going to Connemara God-willing or not!"

And for that piece of heresy, Paddy is turned into a frog and relegated to a frog-pond for several years. When he is allowed to regain his mortal shape, he goes back into his cabin and begins packing up all over again. His friends come back to say goodbye to him and ask: "Where are you going this time Paddy?"

By now, Paddy is more determined than ever. "I'm going to Connemara," he shouts, "or back to the frog-pond!"

I suppose some readers of these strange and wonderful legends will react by saying that they are simply stories any gifted person could invent, but that would not be true. They come from the days when man was himself still a child. He would never be able to dream such bizarre myths today.

The great significance of these samples is, however, that variants have been told thoughout the world—even in Siberia—long before there was any physical communication. This suggests that early man's psychic organism intersected the absolute world, making his consciousness a sensitive apparatus, with esoteric powers to beam thought radiation everywhere in its flow from essence to form.

We ourselves have lost this faculty which operated in such helpful ways for our primitive ancestors. If ever it returns, as it may, we may be able to unlock the chains that bind us. We might be able to broadcast daily, via our telepathic radios, messages of good will and brotherly love to dissident nations.

Since today we do live in a state of doubt, it seems to me an Irish anecdote, which has done duty also in France, Spain, and Finland in varied form, seems apt.

A rider on horseback is lost in the hinterland of Ireland. There are no road signs and he is trying to find his way back to Dublin, but is lost. He comes across a peasant tilling his soil. "Can you please tell me the way to Dublin?" he asks.

With grave courtesy the peasant replies, "I am sorry, sir, I do not know the way to Dublin. But I do know that everyone who comes from the direction in which you are going, tells me they have been to Dublin."

THE HAUNTED ETHER

Strictly speaking, Thomas Edison was not so much an original inventor as he was a synthesizing genius for perfecting the ideas which had been begun by others—with the exception of the phonograph and the incandescent lamp bulb. It was Edison who made the telephone of Alexander Graham Bell so serviceable to mankind. The sound waves of the human voice came through very indistinctly—until Edison improved the telephone to the point where it became commercially important. His triumphs over seemingly insurmountable difficulties of other inventors won him the title of wizard.

He was not a spiritualist, but in old age was inspired to work on an electronic device to augment mediumship, or do away with its use altogether. In his own words, it was to be a "divining instrument which will serve to establish intercommunications between our world and the next."

When a Russian scientist named Vlasimir Durov announced

he had detected thought waves to the length of 1.8 millimeters during telepathic experiments in 1923, Edison became convinced that human thought could, conceivably, continue after death. He began work on his boldest project which was to be "a sort of valve which will increase hundreds of times whatever vibrations are in the ether. It will be so delicate that, if there are personalities in another sphere who wish to contact the living, this ought to give them a better vibration than psychical mediumship offers."

The task Edison set for himself was, of course, to attract the psychic energy taken into the beyond, to capture posthumous thoughts created without the use of a physical brain. He was well aware there are only two known wavelengths—those which are either long or short—but somewhere in between he hoped to find one in which posthumous mental processes can be broadcast. After much work in this device, Edison said in an interview he gave *Liberty* Magazine in 1924, that he had picked up voices from the void. He died before he could perfect his telephone between two worlds.

However, the recent experiments of Dr. Raudive in Germany, and Dr. Jurgenson in Sweden, with tape recordings on which the voices of discarnate voices have been manifested on playbacks of tapes which were unused before, goes to show that obviously Edison was ahead of his time. Dr. Raudive has been joined by many other scientists and electronic engineers—even theologians—in his enthusiasm. The voices made captive on these tapes always speak much slower than in normal speech, using a curious rhythmical effect which seems to be stressing that they are not of this world.

Besides Edison, another great inventor, Guglielmo Marconi (1874-1937) was working in his retirement on a highly sophisticated radio receiver with which he hoped to capture cadences of the past still in the ether. Basing his invention on the known fact that all sound is dynamic and never truly dies, he hoped to isolate sentences uttered by people on earth. In this way he might have recaptured words that were never written down, thus tapping knowledge from great thinkers. Being a devout Roman Catholic, he prayed that he might bring back the words Jesus spoke on the cross.

The immediate difficulties he met were due to the fact that sound waves travel upward sharply, always away from the surface of the earth. In the days when Marconi was working on his device, no electronic power was strong enough to bring them down. He failed, but not without proving a point of interest about the universe. He discovered there are zones of silence in the outer atmosphere where sound dissolved or does not register at all. Had Marconi lived longer (he was dead at 63), with his genius for developing electro-magnetic waves, he might have overcome the handicaps.

Like Marconi, some of our astronauts have been attracted to the psychic aspects of their vocation, notably Ed Mitchell whose whole life has been changed metaphysically by his experience in space. His own psychic ability has helped him to put into words what was formerly outside the range of earthly experience. For him the heavens have become more and more majestic.

The unmanned spaceship, Pioneer 11, is now on its way into the incredible reaches of outer space. It will travel two billion miles to Saturn, where it is scheduled to arrive on September 5, 1979. This amazing feat makes speculation abound for the future of space exploration. If it arrives safely, Pioneer 11 will be one light-hour away from the earth—that is to say, if its camera were powerful enough to photograph a scene on earth, the picture would be of an event which had happened one hour earlier! And so I will now take a few terrific liberties and "crystal-ball" that one day it may be possible to launch and position an exceedingly powerful optical camera on a star 200 light-years away from us.

We know that light from earth reaching that star, and the camera, would have been traveling 200 years and the events photographed would have lived that long in spatialized time. Among the ghostly scenes this camera could snap in 1976 would be some of those for which the year 1776 is famous. We could have the first photographs of the siege of Boston, which ended in March of that year. Or we could, perhaps, be shown details of Washington's brilliant victories at Trenton and Princeton. We might even be given a "still" of the Battle of Bunker Hill.

Now to fantasize in reverse, let us suppose that there is a race of planetary people, far more intelligent than ours, on a star one hundred light-years away. Let us suppose that the optic nerve of these people has far greater sensitivity to grapple with light radiations than ours would and, accordingly, would have much greater vision—also that telescopic power would be perfected beyond our knowledge to enable the astronomer to observe our earth in finest details.

Suppose this astronomer was examining Gettysburg on November 13th, 1963, he would have to see Lincoln delivering a talk back in 1863 which would inspire many generations to come. Or if London on February 10th, 1940, he would be able to revel vicariously in the marriage festivities of Queen Victoria to her cousin, the Prince of Saxe-Coburg.

MECHANISMS OF THE AURA

A story they tell in Dublin illustrates forcibly how easily misunderstandings can develop. A local wag was seated in the lobby of the Shelbourne Hotel next to a rather fierce-looking lady. The long-haired vogue for young men had just begun, getting off to a slow start in Ireland, as most fashions do. A young "hippie" type passed by and nodded to the lady, who smiled back with such civility as to make her appear more friendly than at first glance. So the wag struck up a conversation, commenting sarcastically that it was becoming increasingly difficult to tell the gender of young people. "What a mess that young man looks, anyway!" he added.

"I'm sorry you said that," replied the lady indignantly. "That 'young man' happens to be my daughter!"

"Oh, pray forgive me," said the embarrassed Irishman. "If I had known you are the mother, I would have been more tactful."

"There you go again," snapped the character. "I happen to be the father!"

How infectious is the attitude of ironical sneering. It has become a habit, a fashion, even a system today. Multiplication of it amongst ourselves can lead to personal negation.

Personality aura-variation between human beings is often tremendous and causes a psychic reaction which cannot be explained any other way. But we may be missing a chance to learn a new view of life because we misunderstand or dislike someone we meet briefly, and this congeals them. Every new person we meet can offer interesting views, very different from our own, enabling us to see life's problems in special ways, if given the chance. The way to a sound inner life is to cultivate flexibility of mind and imaginative sympathy in judging others. Have you noticed that friends, commenting on mutual acquaintances, see in those they dislike defects that are definitely not present?

When you take an instant dislike to someone, this attitude (deserved or not) takes root in your subconscious. It remains there until "exorcised" and is likely to become reactivated whenever you meet or think of them. Since you have not taken the trouble to try to find this person's good points—and everyone has a few—he brings you pain instead of pleasure. There is a subconscious desire to avoid this person and you may even feel regret when you hear good news about him!

Personality conflicts are sometimes due to biochemical differences and for that reason you may not be able to put the cause of your dislike into words. If and when you develop all the supernormal faculties within you, however, you will find yourself a far more integral part of the social world. I am not, of course, suggesting that we should try to love everyone, which would obviously become exhausting—especially if everyone loved us in return! The point I am trying to make is that the distinctive mark of a cultured mind is to show interest in others.

For the average person with whom you converse, their world is the only one they know. Egotistical persons are forever believing that they are the center of everyone else's circle. This is especially true of so-called celebrities, who have an infuriating way continually of talking about themselves and never asking a polite question of others. They do not empathize, have little or no time for lasting friendships, and finally wonder why they end their careers alone. The Motion Picture Country Home near Hollywood is filled with "big-name" examples.

Many unimportant personalities have their own systematized approach to art, to love, to marriage, business, and so on. When a subject is broached, they merely play back past thoughts. Whether you agree or not is unimportant to them. It is unlikely they will give you an idea to think about. If only such persons would study themselves within, they might find their own consciousness something which is not strictly their own and which would reveal to them a quality higher than they knew they possessed.

We are very rarely going to find perfection in people. The so-called perfect companion is hardly ever perfect. Show me the man whose wife and off-springs do not secretly think him something of a fool. Mark Twain said of his father that, from the age of fourteen to twenty, he regarded his "old Man" as an awful old dullard. When he reached maturity, however, he was amazed how much his father had learned in those few intervening years!

Admittedly some psychic assaults wound more than others. To be misunderstood by those we love is one of the sadnesses of the inner life. This may account for the tragic subtleties seen in the portraits of many great men, especially Abraham Lincoln. If you suffer derelictions from those close to you, console yourself with the fact that no project, however noble, is without handicaps and hindrances caused by suspicious people. The high places where complete cooperation would be so helpful, such as at conferences of peace or politics, are usually centers of animosity and lack of unification.

Take heart in the statement by the great Pascal, who said that if everyone told everyone else the unpleasant remarks made about them, there would be no friends in all the world. We all speak candidly behind each other's backs, but not necessarily maliciously. Yet who among us cannot recall the psychic impact felt when we discover we have been attacked by someone we thought had been our bosom friend. I myself have found all too often that a "bosom friend" can become all bosom and no friend!

Perhaps, though, we need a few enemies to keep us going. The enemy instinct is lurking in every human heart and the best we can do is to circumscribe it as much as possible. I do not doubt that some of my readers are so gifted with intuition they can read a character at a glance. The majority of us must, however, rely on first impressions which are often dangerously deceptive. Remember the face is not always the mirror of the mind. Human consciousness, which is actually the history of our racial growth, is made up of a vast number of thoughts and feelings; whereas the number of facial muscles to express them is only fifty-two. A combination of these must be used to express the many states of mind and this involves a considerable margin for error. A scowl may express doubt, curiosity, worry, or even a nervous disorder. Or it may reflect misgiving, wonder, or great surprise.

Let's be sure who are our enemies and let us deal with them in such a way that we can draw upon them as a source of psychic strength. When I was a boy at school in England I read an amusing story about two shipwrecked sailors who were forced to live for nearly a year on an island. There was precious little vegetation but much sea-kale, plus wild birds that were difficult to catch. Yet they managed to survive for a year before help came, although they were in very poor shape.

Sometime later, the two men decided to take some rabbits and leave them on the island in order to help any future castaways. Some years afterwards, when some other ship-wrecked seamen were rescued, they were found in a far worse condition although they had only been on the island a month. It was now strewn with masses of decaying rabbit corpses and all the vegetation had been eaten by them before they died. Without their natural enemies to keep their population in check, the rabbits had bred more rapidly than the island's resources could feed them.

So with us, enemies are a necessity in the worldly scheme of things. Why let human malignity or ingratitude enrage us? Apart from the religious device of forgiveness, the wisest course is to form in your mind a "forgettry." This is accomplished by putting into reverse the advice of the experts on memory. They advise that we concentrate on what we want to remember and find a link for it with other matters uppermost in your mind. There you have the essential rules for forgetting. To banish a grievance, or an unpleasant experience, do not concentrate on it. Try not to link it with anything else to which it might be compared. Send the matter into your "Forgettry" and it will be devoured.

But, as counterpoise to enemies, every once in a lifetime someone enters our lives whose eminent qualities throw off a prodigious luster for us. They appear as if from nowhere, like one of those new stars that baffle scientists, bring us much joy—and then, to our unspeakable sorrow, disappear from sight. There can be no substitution for these people, who open the floodgates of our inner consciousness and bring out what is poetic in us. We must reserve our finest thought-radiation for them while they are of this world.

In life, soul must judge soul, testing the psychic chemistry to see if it is attuned and when found, the precious link should never be broken. The more we radiate kindliness with our aura, the more it will be bestowed upon us. It is like an invisible currency, the main value of which comes from its spending. Often it will be returned by someone you least expect. Even when you love someone who is unable to return the affection, you will find another love born in its place.

THE BURIED RELIC

At the close of a sultry summer's day in 1907, when the sunlight was slowly fading from the sky, a gathering of exceptional interest took place at Fulham Palace, the residence of the Bishop of London. It consisted of about fifty persons including ministers of various religions, scientists, antiquaries and also the American Ambassador.

The audience was addressed by an American, a tall athletic type of man by the name of Mr. Tudor Pole. He explained that he was the head of the London branch of a large American firm, and up to the time of the incident he was about to relate, he had not been aware of possessing any kind of clairvoyance other than that of being clear-sighted in business.

In a corner of the room where he was speaking, there lay a little case which held a glass vessel of quite unique shape, rather like a Eucharistic chalice, but lower and wider. It was of a greenish-blue color, and from a distance it looked as if the artist who created it had introduced a subtle ornamentation of almost imperceptible silverleaf which shone softly in the lamplight.

Collectors and connoisseurs among those present had examined the vase and declared that they were unable to trace its origin or to identify the period to which it belonged. Some suggested that it might be late Phoenecian while others felt that its archaic dignity pointed rather to the most ancient period of Venetian glass manufacture. All agreed that the mysterious object was a work of grace and beauty.

Mr. Pole proceeded to explain that at the beginning of the year 1902 he was returning home one evening, his brain full of calculations and figures, when suddenly an internal force of an indefinable kind surged up in him emanating from nowhere and holding him enthralled for a very brief period of time. During this interval he received a direct impression that somewhere near the town of Glastonbury (of which he knew only because he had passed through it by train) there lay buried a relic of the most sacred kind. He did not pay much

67

attention to this odd impression, and after a while he forgot all about it.

It was not until the end of 1906 that the impression again flashed through his mind, and this time a distinct voice spoke to him, reminding him more and more strongly that the holy relic near Glastonbury was waiting for his discovery.

The strange impression occurred more often now. It attained its strongest urge in the month of November when he saw at least three times a day with his mind's eye the detailed picture of a spot half a mile distant from Glastonbury Abbey where the relic was buried by a small spring in a pool. It was as though he were dreaming with his eyes wide open, for these impressions always came in the daytime.

Mr. Pole's many occupations prevented him from going himself to the spring to look for the relic and get rid of his obsession. So he sent his sister who thought of the expedition as a pleasant weekend trip and decided to invite two friends to come along with her. The three ladies, to their great surprise, did find the pool and the spring at a place known as Bride's Hill, and under a large stone which had protected it from injury and human observation, the rainbow-colored sacred vessel which had been indicated by the voice in Mr. Pole's mysterious daydreams.

The ladies did not dare to carry away the chalice and concealed it again under the stone. Upon their return they informed Mr. Pole of what had happened and he in turn went at once to see his vicar who was exceedingly interested in the whole affair, and together the two gentlemen went to Glastonbury and fetched the vase.

Word about the discovery reached the Bishop of London who, being somewhat of an antiquarian himself, arranged the meeting of experts at his home.

The evening discussion remained of course inconclusive, but the account of it received quite a play in the London papers. It made an excellent news story even though no one could foresee that the most fascinating part of it was yet to come. Mr. Pole was going over the newspapers after returning home a few evenings later when the maid announced that a certain Dr. Goodchild wished to see him. A rather learned type of man appeared who, looking him straight in the face, said to Mr. Pole: "I have just read of your discovery of the chalice at Glastonbury. It was I who put it in the spring at Bride's Hill several years ago."

He then went on to explain that he had been a professor at a Welsh university from which post he had retired some time ago. Then he unfolded the romantic incidents that led up to his depositing the relic in the spring.

For many years he had been in the habit of passing his summers on the Riviera. In 1885, a friend who knew of his passion for porcelain and glass vases informed him that there was for sale, in a curiosity shop at Bordighera, an antique vase which looked like a very rare type. He went at once to the shop and purchased it for 150 francs.

Dr. Goodchild gave the vase as a gift to his father in England and had almost forgotten about its existence when seventeen years later a curious psychological experience befell him. One day in September, 1902, he was about to leave his home when he fell into a trance in which a strange form appeared to him. The trance was so obfuscating that he did not remember any visual details of the apparition, but the words it had uttered were very intelligible and had been repeated several times. Dr. Goodchild understood that he was somehow in great danger, for the cup he had bought seventeen years earlier at Bordighera was the "Cup of Our Lord" which He had used at the Last Supper; it was to be taken immediately to some holy ground and be hidden there; at a particularly distressful time for the Faith, it would eventually be removed and would be used in some way for the propagation of the faith of Jesus Christ.

Dr. Goodchild complied with the instructions given him and took the chalice to Glastonbury because he could think of no holier spot in all England. Now that it had been rediscovered, what should be done?

The two men decided to offer it to the Vatican, where it seemed to belong. However, inspection by London Roman Catholic officials gave the quietus to that course. It was decided that the chalice was not nearly old enough to have been used by Jesus. No one tried to explain the agency that had seen fit to use Dr. Goodchild and Mr. Tudor Pole as its messengers and the whole affair fell into the limbo of forgotten things.

POSTHUMOUS PAINTING

Robert Swain Gifford was an American scenic artist of some note who died in 1905. Many of his landscapes hang in museums throughout America and represent the artist's love of New England. A posthumous exhibit was held in the latter part of January 1906, at the American Art Galleries in New York City. A certain Mr. J.L. Thompson who was a goldsmith, went to see the exhibit because he remembered having sold Mr. Gifford some jewelry years before and somehow he was interested in his late client's talent.

While looking admiringly at the paintings a voice came into his ears repeating like a gramophone record: "You see what I have done . . . You must take up and finish my work . . . You see what I have done . . . You must take up and finish my work . . ." There followed strange visions of twisted old trees whose leaves appeared to tremble with secret horror, set against a storm-wracked sky. The pale orb of the moon emitted luminous streams of light on two black windmills in the distance, one with gigantic motionless sails and the other wingless, and both of them almost eclipsed by the gnarled trees. Mr. Thompson was unable to understand the meaning of these visions although he realized that they had deep allegorical significance, giving the impression of a human being in haste and panic.

Mr. Thompson became so conscious of all this that he could not go on with his work. The voice and the visions cast a cloud over his whole life. Finally his wife took him to see a psychiatrist who recommended that he be sent to an institution.

In some way his case came to the attention of Professor

James H. Hyslop, a psychologist and specialist in cases of obsession. Dr. Hyslop suggested that Mr. Thompson try to paint the scenes which haunted him hoping through that medium to unpack the patient's mind. Before this time the goldsmith had done some occasional sketching which he had learned in a very elementary art course.

As soon as he put his visions on to canvas his health improved and strangely enough, the paintings proved of such merit that he was advised to show them to the art critic James B. Townsend. This gentleman was so struck by their quality that he bought one at once, and without knowing any of the odd facts that inspired their creator, he remarked that the style reminded him very much of the late Robert Swain Gifford.

Encouraged by the monetary gain but still haunted by the visions of the trees, the budding artist set out in a resolve to verify his apparitions. This he thought would be possible by a trip to Nonquitt, Massachusetts, the summer home of Gifford. He actually went there in July, 1907, and the first thing he did was to call on Mrs. Gifford.

When he had explained the reason for his call, the widow took him into the studio of her husband which had not been used since the artist's death. In a frenzy of surprise Thompson saw on the easel an unfinished painting of trees absolutely identical with those of his vision which he had painted some months before.

Mr. Thompson then went to the island where Mrs. Gifford stated her husband had been painting in the autumn before he died and where a severe storm had interrupted his work the last time he was there.

Wandering about for a half hour or so the visitor came upon the scene of his hallucination. Here were the hoary trees, twisted in horrible convulsions, and in the distance the two mills. Out came his sketch book and just as he put pencil to paper the voice resounded in his ear: "Go and look on the other side of the furthest tree." And on the opposite side of the tree he found the initials "R.S.G. 1902" carved on the bark.

71

All these facts were verified by Dr. Hyslop who states in his book, *Contact with the Other World,* that the initials were aged by several years and could not possibly have been carved by Mr. Thompson. The original paintings by Mr. Gifford and the ones of Mr. Thompson's vision, together with photographs of the scenes are on view at the American Society for Psychical Research in New York City.

THE REVENANT MODEL

Gerald Brockhurst, a member of the coveted English Royal Academy, was once well known for his portraits, especially of the Duchess of Windsor and Marlene Dietrich. He was famed for his gift of getting likenesses with comparatively few sittings. Busy people were pleased to be spared the numerous posing engagements required by other artists.

Brockhurst is of course aided in his accomplishments by a remarkable visual memory and absolute mastery of the techniques of portraiture, but long ago he discovered that certain people—as he likes to describe it—leave behind them an etheric double which can be called upon to pose at any time convenient for the artist and wherever the prototype may happen to be.

The method which Brockhurst uses seems natural enough. He looks at his sitters most attentively, sketching from time to time on the canvas but really fixing in his mind's eye the features so indelibly that they become enshrined in his memory. Then he puts the canvas away and begins another sitter.

Later on he locates the "etheric double," seats it in a chair, and proceeds to paint it just as if the sitter were before him in person. The extraordinary thing now is that the double often appears more vividly than the person in the flesh so that the artist is able to get a better likeness from it than from the sitter himself.

Quite a few years ago, Brockhurst was staying in the picturesque town of Carnac, in Brittany, for the purpose of doing some landscape sketching. He was sitting outside a tavern, having some evening coffee and enjoying the balmy summer air. Moonlight streamed down on the village thoroughfare which was swarming with people. There passed by crowds of tourists and local residents, a conglomeration of well-dressed and for the most part self-sufficient folk.

Suddenly he was struck by the appearance of a young woman. She was really a wisp of a girl, rather slim with a complexion white as milk, set off against very blonde hair and eyebrows; but it was her downcast expression that attracted his notice most particularly. She wore a kerchief round her head which seemed to accentuate her pathetic mood, and she reminded Mr. Brockhurst of one of the tragic heroines of Maeterlinck's plays. The color of her eyes he could not see for she passed by with determined steps, signifying that she was bound on some important errand.

A few nights later, in his hotel room, Brockhurst thought that he would try to coax his eyes to recall the form and lineaments of this strange little girl whose image he could not forget. So he set himself to picture the pale face, the blonde hair, the pose of the head and neck with a view to sketching her. There, he said to himself, her arm would rest on the elbow of the chair, there her dress.

Unexpectedly, as if his efforts at picturing the image had nothing to do with it, the sad vision appeared before his eyes. For some minutes he sat silent, reveling in the possession of his accomplishment. afraid to move lest the beautiful apparition should fade away forever. Although he was aware that this was no ghost but a simple natural illusion, there was something that distinguished it from the usual materializations which he used for his portrait sitters.

The likeness to the original was absolutely perfect, but what amazed his sensitive observations was the fact that the eyes, which he had never seen, blended into the personality as if nature had created them. The image seemed as if it would like to speak and move about, but it remained utterly still.

As Mr. Brockhurst sat entranced he heard footsteps

outside and a knock at the door. Opening it he found the proprietor's wife with a telegram for him, and as she handed it through the half-open door, she looked in the direction of the chair where the image was seated, and gave a most perceptible start. Then she took her leave with a suspicious glance at the artist. Was it possible, he asked himself, that his dream picture had become a spatial reality for the eyes of another?

At once the pallor of the girl gave way to an indignant blush, as if she were embarrassed at being found in a man's room unchaperoned. After a few minutes Mr. Brockhurst felt embarrassed, too, and instead of beginning to draw, he dissolved the image and went out for a walk.

Next day he was visited by a local gendarme. In a peremptory manner he asked: "Where is Mlle Leclerc? She has been missing from her home and was seen in this room by the proprietress last night."

Mr. Brockhurst was at a loss as to how to explain his position. Investigations continued for some hours, and fortunately the evidence absolving him was not long in being brought to light. The body of Mlle Leclerc was found at the bottom of a steep and lonely cliff along the coast. She had committed suicide on the night he chose to sketch her.

SECTION THREE

E.S.P. AND PLANT LIFE

Mysterious senses of the plant world have been attracting attention recently with best-selling books on the subject. The man who first discovered how to utilize the psychic life of plants was Luther Burbank (1849-1926). True his fame rests on the potato which bears his name—the parent of all the best potatos grown everywhere today. He originated it through his gifts of clairvoyance and telepathy.

This outstanding American was suggestible to psychic influences at an early age. In her book about him, his sister, Emma Burbank Beeson, tells of the time when, as a baby, he playfully upset a potted cactus plant and was badly pricked by the spines. Much later in his life, he tried to develop the thornless cactus but significantly, as we shall see, this was one of his few failures in horticulture.

As Burbank was growing up he read avidly. Accidentally he came across a book which told about a plant in Italy named the Rose of Jericho. It is a hardy, known in most warm climates as the field daisy. It bears a white flower similar to the daisy, but this one is unique. In dry seasons, when the earth is devitalized and only sand is left in which to survive, it shows uncanny adaptation by separating itself from such inhospitable soil. Flower, root and stem, it wraps itself into a ball-like shape, so it may be carried by the wind until it reaches a more suitable habitat, where it takes root again.

Luther's boyish imagination saw by this illustration that all life is a process of opportunistic adaptation in which those plants that fail become extinct. In this poetic example of the Jericho Rose he saw a soul in all plant life, one imbued with intelligence as clever, in this instance, as any human being. In a sudden flash of clairvoyance he realized that he would himself outgrow the sands of formalism wherein he was currently enmeshed. He knew that sooner or later he would have to detach himself from the old-fashioned ways in which his native state in New England was steeped. He visualized himself ultimately trekking Westward to California.

He had always had the gift of second-sight. One day when he and his parents were marketing, they returned to find a valuable piece of farm equipment had been damaged by trespassers. The young Luther told his father exactly how it had occurred. He said that boys from a neighboring farm (who had trespassed on the Burbank property before), had been over and had tried to run the new plow, which was easy to misuse. He even gave the names of the guilty boys.

The elder Burbank felt he could not possibly have any knowledge such as he proclaimed and chastized his son for inventing the story. Running to his mother, the child wept profusely insisting he had seen all this while it was happening. She consoled him, telling him that she, too, could "see" certain events while miles away. She warned him that he must try to keep this faculty under control or it would cause misunderstandings. Next day Luther's vision was verified and his father apologized to him.

He always insisted, after he became world-famous, that he had inherited his psychic gifts from his mother. One day while plowing on his father's potato patch, his sixth sense sent his hand into the earth amidst a clump of potatoes. To his great astonishment and joy he brought out a huge seedball, the rarest of agricultural prizes. He knew enough to realize his treasure-trove because his teacher at Lancaster Academy in Massachusetts had just told him that normal potatoes do not make any seeds. They propagate by means of the "eyes" of their tubers. At once he took the seed ball to his teacher who congratulated him for finding a specimen hitherto unknown in the district.

Of course Burbank planted the seedball which produced a record crop of twenty-three potato plants, all of which yielded different varieties. This was a revolution in potato culture, for which he became locally famous. He selected the best variety and named it "The Burbank." This led him to start a seed farm in Lunenburg, his hometown, which he ran for over a year.

In his first real hot-house, he discovered that most plants have sense organs as sensitive as any human being's. He noted how they imbibe food, drink, digest, respond to differing temperatures, and accommodate themselves to light and darkness. Moreover, he was struck by the fact that they have the same susceptibilities as human beings. They suffer fatigue, have nervous breakdowns and can become "drunk" when too much water is taken. They have memories, too. If they are subjected to an unseasonal piece of cold weather, it takes a plant several days to "forget" the experience. Their leaves droop until the shock to the system gradually disappears.

All this came to him largely through psychic perception, but it showed his friends that he was a born plant developer. What he needed now was a place to work where soil conditions would not be so seasonal and where he could work all the year round. So, imitating the plant he first admired that wrapped itself into a ball and traveled, he decided to transplant himself to faraway California.

After much prospecting on the West Coast, he decided upon Santa Rosa in Sonoma Valley not far from San Francisco. Here he built the house where he lived until he died.

Coincident with his arrival was the American publication in 1875 of Charles Darwin's *The Effects of Cross-Fertilization and Self-Fertilization in the Vegetable Kingdom,* which attracted his full attention. This was a meticulous study of what today is called the sex life of plants. It became Burbank's bible. He grasped the message quickly, that all life has within it three powers, which are inherent:—the power to fight for existence, the power to reproduce and the power to vary. For Darwin life is a dynamic process that will never be completed.

The need for more lumber suggested to him the mass production of trees. He saw in the tree a similar physical organization to that of man. The tree has a mind and it thinks with it. It has a circulation system that uses sap instead of blood. It uses leaves for lungs. Its skin we call bark. Burbank believed that all trees converse and whisper to each other. In sharing a common soil, they reach out and touch others under the earth. He saw in trees all that there is in man, in a purer, less visible form.

With such empathy he was able to find the vulnerable spot in nature which every one else had missed. It made her his co-worker! He produced the largest hybrid walnut tree ever known, twice the size of any other. He developed new varieties of prunes, peaches, quince, apple, and a hybrid he named the plumcot.

With mounting success, he extended his laboratories to Sebastapol, California, where he crossbred innumerable flowers. The rose attracted him for a singular reason. He was aware that the hips of this ancient plant have been known as long ago as Elizabethan times for their high food value. He thought of mass-producing them as fodder for cattle. At that time he had no way of knowing that they were also very rich in Vitamin C. This fact was established (long after his death) by the Royal Botanic Gardens at Kew, England.

An interesting discovery he made was that some flowering plants time their lives by internal "clocks." Certain flowers he studied know precisely when the sun is going to rise and open exactly an hour beforehand. Even when these flowering plants are kept in complete darkness for a week the flowers open as if they were out-of-doors.

It was this preternatural endowment of the sixth-sense, supplemented by a thorough knowledge of horticulture, that brought Luther Burbank recognition as a wizard. Just as he telepathized pictorial messages to his mother until she died, so he sent his plants thought telegrams—assuring them of his love and appreciation. He would also hold whispered conversations with some of his flowers and they would respond by showing off a brighter bloom.

His gifts of telepathy were tested in 1920 at the Department of Psychology in Stanford University, where he lectured twice yearly on horticulture. (This department was carrying out investigations into E.S.P. long before Dr. Rhine at Duke University.) It was found that Burbank was able to use telepathy almost as satisfactorily as the telephone! He received seven messages "broadcast" out of ten. This was his average on several testings.

Of course, he had his failures in using E.S.P. in plants. One was with the cactus, which he wanted to breed spineless so that it could be used as fodder for cattle. This hardy succulent has survived hardships since time immemorial, making it a stubborn creature to try to vary. Actually, it grew its spines originally for protection against being devoured by animals.

"You don't need to be defensive any more," he lied, to the selected specimens. "I am Luther Burbank. I will protect you!"

But the plants would not be fooled. He did succeed in breeding a few generations without spines, but they grew back eventually as thorny as ever. In this instance he failed to nudge the evolutionary laws of nature. Dame Nature hit back!

Honors were showered upon him in old age. Burbank was now as famous as Henry Ford and Thomas Edison. School children were taken in droves for glimpses of him in his fields. A lucky visitor to Santa Rosa or Sebastapol would see the great plant-developer striding along a row of seedlings at a fast pace, even when he was reaching seventy. Every now and then he would tell an assistant to make a special marking on a certain plant he had selected. He was uncanny in this selection. Doubting persons who would try to cultivate his rejections always found him correct.

In his seventy years attendance at what he called The University of Nature, he declared that his success was due to his insatiable curiosity, occult powers, and horticultural knowledge. Indeed, as a man he was inseparable from nature. She collaborated with him more than other experts in their hot-house laboratories. They would sweat interminably over a handful of experimental records on cross-fertilization, whereas Burbank would deal with thousands of plants in very short order.

In an interview with Mrs. Burbank, which she graciously gave me in 1953, I asked her whether it was true that her late husband was an atheist. She replied "The inhabitants of the horticultural world taught my husband that their support comes from a source higher than the world in which they have their being, so they turn towards the light whenever they can. Burbank knew from the start that there is no such thing as a petty fact in nature. He recognized that her laws are finely correlated and infallibly just. This proved to him the existence of a Great Authority."

One might say that he saw with the eyes of the spirit. His greatest contribution was opening the door to the future cosmic understanding of the plant world, now being born. The students who follow in his footsteps may yet tell more of the surprises which still remain.

ANIMAL COMMUNICATION

One of the most fascinating fields of extrasensory perception is in animal study. Scientific research to determine how much E.S.P. does exist in our dumb friends is being carried out continuously, especially at the Parapsychology Laboratory of Duke University in North Carolina. A recent statement declared that tests yielded significant results under conditions which make clairvoyance in most animals an established fact.

Professor Bozzano, an important Italian zoologist, published in 1927 a treatise for *Annales Des Sciences Psychiques* in which he cited authenticated cases of dogs, cats, horses, and even geese, involved in subliminal communications with human beings. He anticipated what is now being proved, that nature has equipped many animals with highly sophisticated sense organs which are used for communication.

An Irishman with the odd name of "Humanity Dick" Martin (1745-1834) long ago satisfied himself that he could communicate with many creatures. His portrait is in a place of honor in the Board Room of the Royal Society for the Prevention of Cruelty to Animals, which he founded in London in 1824. It portrays a man in the prime of life with eyes that reflect inward vision. The sensitive curve of the brow is in strange contrast to the square jaw which proclaims determination. To accomplish what he did in his fight to protect animals, he needed all he could muster!

Richard Martin was one of the most remarkable men of his generation. He was known as the uncrowned King of Connemara, which he inherited from his father—an immense rock-strewn moorland and bog in County Galway. There he ruled over a straggling population who lived on market gardening and what they could grab from shipwrecks. The coast is lorded over by the majestic, often furious Atlantic, which accounted for the wreckage.

When a boy he became keenly aware of the emotional sounds of farm animals, those noises which designate warning, challenge, fear, joy, pain or love, also the gestures the animals use among themselves. Once he became on such friendly terms with a gaggle of geese, and so thoroughly understood the cackle of the birds, that he won a place in their flock! He would cackle at them in perfect goose-language and the gaggle would pace their waddling to his changing gait. By studying his geese he found the cackle often "published" a particular piece of information by means of its heightened emotional pitch.

More importantly, he found that some of his pets, such as his dog, cat, or horse, could read his mind, even interpret his inner feelings. He invented his own language for them to obey, composed of certain sounds and cadences which, in the case of his horses, was understood far better than the equivalent utterances, such as "Woo" and the use of the spur. His dog learned over fifty words, made up of invented

81

sounds, which the animal could translate into action.

In order to help the animal kingdom, Richard knew he must enter the slippery domain of politics, which he hated. He got himself elected to Parliament in 1809 for the constituency of Galway, and his work began. In England he was considered an odd character. Most people could not understand, in that cultured but callous period, a man who cared for animals to the extent that he did. But they had to take care because he was an impulsive duelist with appropriate scars to prove it.

In Parliament he made his vigorous personality felt but his attempt to bring in the bills to make the law to protect the "brute creation" was very uphill work. Between the years 1809 and 1820 he brought forward several bills, all of which were mocked with derision at first. One was against ill-treatment of cattle, another against inhumane slaughtering of horses, and still another against bull-baiting. The latter did not pass since it was Prime Minister Canning's favorite sport. In 1824 the first act to protect animals became law.

It provided that any person accused of ill-treating any animal be summoned before a magistrate and be fined five pounds upon conviction or imprisoned for three months. This act is parent to all laws of this type elsewhere in the world. Hundreds of convictions followed. Aware that some of his tenants would be tried and unable to pay a fine, Richard made haste to build a small prison in Connemara, the ruins of which can be seen to this day.

Eventually he was presented to King George IV, who found him amusing with his frothy Irish wit. His Majesty offered to sponsor a society for the prevention of cruelty and in parting said, jokingly "I rechristen you 'Humanity Dick' Martin!" The moniker stuck and this became his new given name.

On July 18, 1825 "Humanity Dick" presided over the first meeting of the Royal Society for the Prevention of Cruelty to Animals. It was held, oddly enough, at Slaughter's Coffee House in St. Martin's Lane. In a speech before the distinguished gathering, Martin said that he found no barrier between animal intelligence and his own. Although he was unable to appreciate thoroughly the psychic powers he used in communication with his pets because they were uncatalogued at that time, he knew he had them. No one had yet dared to be so outspoken about the matter of animal communication. Animals were generally classed as brutes.

The formation of this Society was to have world-wide repercussions. It was soon widely imitated throughout the civilized world, and altered the morals, habits, and thoughts of men everywhere (America was the very last country to join the movement. The American Society was founded in 1866 by a retired diplomat named Henry Bergh, who also prepared the legislation protecting animals—but not until 1886!).

As for "Humanity Dick," the work he had done for animals began telling on his health, also his finances. He had allowed his personal affairs in Ireland to be managed by others, who were incompetent. Debts began mounting and bailiffs seized much of his land. Soon the situation had deteriorated so badly that he was forced to flee his creditors and settle on the Continent. He died many years later, a forgotten figure, living at Boulogne in France on his small pension from Parliament. He left no legacy except a request that his dog and cat should be cared for as long as they lived. Because he had failed financially, the press regarded him as a failure, but his friend, Thomas Moore, the famed Irish poet, saw further. He pronounced his obituary in lapidary language:

"There is now not a cow, a calf, dog, or cat, or hack, but what is not in mourning for our good-hearted "Humanity Dick" Martin."

* * * * * * * * *

Any reader who owns a dog will have evidence of its ESP in one way or another. May I speak of "Master McGrath," the most remarkable Irish Greyhound that ever lived? He was born in Kilkenny in 1875 and died in 1884 of a heart attack. He raced both in Ireland and England, winning thirty-six of his thirty-seven races.

McGrath had benefited, as do all Greyhounds born in

Ireland, from the grasslands rich in limestone, which gave him a superb skeletal structure. He was thirty-two inches in height and weighed 127 pounds. He had a large handsome head, small, pointed ears—showing evidence of his ancestry from the ancient Irish wolf-hound. Coloring was in black and white patches here and there. A chest as wide and consistent with great speed and a broad, powerful back gave the finishing touch of a master Greyhound.

This dog seemed to use sight more than scent in pursuit of the prey during a race. He seldom barked but used instead a noise which varied between a yelp and a whine. A few days after McGrath died, his owner, a Patrick Fitzherbert, died too. The *Irish Times* summed up the life of Master McGrath in a glowing obituary. "This amazing Irishman," it stated, "proved that dogs share with us some of the mental attributes which are considered exclusively human . . ." Another paper published a piece of doggerel verse remembering McGrath in action:

The hare she led on to a wonderful view
And swift as the wind cross the meadows she flew
McGrath jumped on her back, then held up a paw
"Three cheers for old Ireland," he cried with guffaw.

INSPIRATION FROM SCENERY

The Amerind still obtains most of his mystical inspiration from Nature. He sees intelligence everywhere—speech in trees, sermons in escarpments, music in the elements—even when they are angry. For certain tribes no notations are used for music, only an ideograph is needed for a song—from which any member can sing at sight. Neither is there a word in any vocabulary for wilderness, because for the Amerind, what we call "wild" is a form of companionship. Go with any Redman to a primeval sight and you will see how he can divine its messages from the beckoning silences.

I believe the most haunted scenery in America is to be found at the Grand Canyon of the Colorado—the most stupendous wonder of the world! This area of natural phenomena is filled with pure magic. Here amid weird erosion formations resembling minarets, pagodas, Grecian pillars, cathedral spires, etc.—all in dazzling colors—menacing forms seemingly envelop, rather than touch, the visitor. In certain places the erosions take on attitudes of sinister violence, and it was probably here where pagan rituals of worship took place, with all the cruel practices of those faraway times.

The Canyon's vast dimensions make it overwhelming, but gradually the chaotic immensity takes on an harmonious whole as one absorbs the stark fact that here is architecture which no group of human geniuses could invent or imitate satisfactorily. One feels that the Amerinds were right in deciding that it is the most perfect place for worshipping the Divine Intelligence. For these ancient erosions seem to be saying that they represent an eternal present in which they have no past—only a future which stretches into a very distant posterity. In their lapidary stillness one feels they will always be there, long after our race has disappeared.

I write the above because we all have within us our own kaleidoscope with which to interpret a piece of scenery. No one person can see the same scenery exactly as another. Pastoral countryside can be for one a Beethoven symphony and, for a farmer, merely a good harvest. Like life itself, scenery is viewed through the spectrums of many eyesights. How differently we ourselves see things at twenty, forty, or sixty.

For the philosopher, every landscape has its particular soul which can be caressing and maternal. Like the human soul it must be divined by opening the ears to its verbal melody, as well as visually. Almost all great writers and composers have drawn inspiration from natural scenery. By reaching out to the cosmic power it offers, their work has been invigorated.

How well I remember a walk I once took with the late Lord Dunsany, the Irish poet-mythologist, in the Wicklow Hills near Dublin. As we both gazed on a beautiful prospect, with the green carpet below adorned by the shadows of

85

passing clouds, my heart opened with a breathtaking gasp.

"You can't have that scene," snapped the eccentric Irish genius, "It belongs to me!"

At first perplexed, I finally got his point. Possession is what we hold in our hands; whereas ownership is what we keep in our memories. We truly only own what we can embrace with a spiritual attachment. This was the secret of Dunsany's poetic gift. He always tried to see in whatever he wrote about further than anyone else had seen, so that he really "owned" it. This is, of course, the magic wand of every good poet. They make themselves bankers of beautiful memories!

Lord Dunsany had a theory that we are all born with a subconscious knowledge of our own lands. My knowledge of Ireland is a familiarity which is not inevitable because I was not born there, yet wherever I go in the Emerald Isle I feel I know it thoroughly. I have rested on ancient cairns and gazed on former battlefields, perhaps fought over by my kinsmen in times of pre-history. I have felt that same *déjà vu* knowledge in gentle Connemara, where vista upon vista of sea and bog and sky and mountains woo the eyes for many a mile.

Whenever you become tired of the world's disgraces, repair to your nearest sights of nature. You who live near mountains lift up your eyes to them whenever you can. Let your thoughts sail onwards until they mingle with the cosmos and your mind merges from finite reality to infinite bliss. Visit your mountains in winter, when snow gives them an ermine charm—when the trees themselves seemingly belong to another creation in which white has taken the place of green.

Or if your home is near the sea, make a visit to its shores at every opportunity throughout the year. Observe its many moods, sometimes threatening or just lingering. Veined with green and drab in winter, she can change from translucent blue to amethyst in summer. Always about her business, she is making clouds, heaping up her sands, visiting her endless shores and bathing them with foam white as milk. Above all, she is feeding the universal life in all its forms.

Find the companionship which this mother of all waters offers with her crested waves, perpetually in motion. Gaze on those brooding headlands, etherialized in the distance and resembling a succession of ghosts. Watch the "skyscapes" for wind and storm, bringing their own kind of beauty, as well as optical phenomena.

Is there any more stunningly beautiful arch than the rainbow, welcoming the return of the sun? It is nature's finest psychic phenomenon in all its colors, symmetry, and general magnitude. The ancient Greeks created a goddess in honor of it and called her Iris. Or, at any eventide, lose yourself in reverie by following the incomparable tracks of gold as the sun sinks into the horizon and traces its route upon the wrinkled water.

No one has to go far out of town to find trees. Any forest offers a spiritualizing experience or just to relax taut nerves. Along any journey, notice the trees in varied and imposing forms. Some dart into the heavens as if they were astronaut rockets ready for shooting into space, while others are arranged in battle formation. Still others raise lonely, phantom-like peaks, in isolated places. Dawn and evening cast a perfecting light upon them, suggesting that they have been left there by some absent-minded god.

Who can stand unmoved amid the majestic tree shapes at the Californian National Parks, such as Sequoia? Here you step into a world of silence and pine-scented air, forgotten by bustling time. You cannot see their like anywhere else in the world, not even in Syria, where the Cedars of Lebanon were once the greatest of sights. Both the Lebanese and the American were mature when the Egyptians were building their pyramids.

Remember that natural scenery is like anything else in life—you get out of it what you bring to it. It always offers unsuspected resources for engaging the eyes and the soul, but you must bring your receptive best to it. Spiritual appreciation of these sights is rather like developing a photographic film. There is no way of telling if it has been exposed until subjected to a chemical process, and its great defect is that it has not been "thought." To fully appreciate the psychic aspects of landscape, a scene must be placed upon the sensitive lens of the third eye. You probably have hundreds of these photos in your subconscious which only need "developing."

You will learn, if not already, that nature speaks a thousand languages. She is always saying to you "Come and find me. I have enough for all!" In scenes of natural grandeur you become enfranchised in spirit, freed from all sense of space and time. On all sides stretch marvels without limit and without end.

Follow the seasons and watch what progress Spring is making. Delightful surprises await you in any garden. At the corner of the walk, half hidden under a shrub, you may find a small-leaved corolla. What spring-like innocence, what soft and modest loveliness, there is in a little flower, opening gently to the sun like a smile. Or if you live in places where succulents flourish, explosions of the Star of Bethlehem and other passion flowers, appear to ravish the eyes. A modest garden contains more instruction than a similar library if we know how to see. And we must learn to look before we can expect to see!

The easiest out-of-the-body experience is only a few feet away from your front door. Look up at the sky any night when it is clear and observe the stars wandering in the pale moonlight. Like a ship, in this ocean of blue, our planet is floating! Surrender your mind to this heavenly spectacle by sight of the infinite from the vantage of the finite. Do this whenever you feel in the need of self-renewal.

Apart from the aura found in natural scenery, there is the subconscious beauty to be discovered in an ancient town. An old market town offers a subconscious familiarity because the inhabitants have usually come from long descent of the original settlers and are more psychically intact than in larger towns. Your psyche finds it easy to understand the thought-atmosphere of the place and makes it possible for some people to remember being there before. In a first visit to any new place, try to penetrate as far as possible into the psychic life of the town and its personalities. Feel it live as your intuitions become more and more distinct. Let the town belong temporarily to you, as you refresh your soul with a formerly unknown existence. In short, let sight pass into vision and gather a harvest of images to take away with you. All this can make you sensible to the difference between yourself and the great majority of travelers.

What a therapy for the increasing neuroticism of these times, but whoever heard of a psychiatrist prescribing great scenery or a visit to an ancient town? Yet such communion restores the intensity of life and can also reveal one to oneself. Fees are, of course, more certain if your psychiatrist keeps you nearer to his office!

Using visits to new scenes for developing the inner life, a new sense of poise will be felt. Seek beauty and repose will come, sounds trite, but it is said very truly by the maximist. In fact, our own little lives can be compared to the four seasons of nature's laboratory. If the flowers of youth have to vanish, never to return, the summers, autumns, and winters can have their own majestic grandeur—with every age having its own particular compensations. Algernon Swinburne, the great English poet, preferred to liken his life to a weary, but picturesque, river yearning for the sea. This helped him smooth out the wrinkles in his soul.

So we can think of ourselves aboard a launch winding through dangerous rapids and beautiful waterfalls—passing rich valleys of verdure along the banks. Watch out for the deceptive mud-flats wherein it is easy to become waylaid. Look forward to the peaceful lakes en route where now and then you can find rest. At the estuary begins the open sea—the great adventure which can soar as high as its furthest longing and unimaginable repose.

INTUITIONS OF EMOTIONS

While visiting the Old Abbey Theater in Dublin before it was consumed by fire, I attended a performance of a new comedy by Lennox Robinson, who was known as the dramatist of Irish discontent. I arrived nearly half an hour late and the audience was already captive—laughing enthusiastically at the amusing lines. At once I found myself entering into the ambience although I knew nothing of what had gone before.

I was, of course, experiencing the mass thought-transference created at any gathering. When large numbers of persons get together, the tendency is for the psychism to draw everyone the same direction, regardless of the original purpose that united them. It is well known that large groups of people do not think or act as they would separately—a fact that successful playwrights have been aware of since the Greeks.

What interested me was the way my aura was blending nicely with the others in the audience, which was made up of different stratas of Irish society as well as foreigners—for Ireland is "internationalized" now like any other European city compared with when Yeats and Lady Gregory started the Abbey Theater.

To put it psychically we had established a collective state of mind. Even the cast was responding to this happy situation, and it was brought home to me that the emotions of people in any group are exceedingly contagious. We all run into difficulties when we tell jokes to smaller groups of people and we wonder what makes one person laugh at one, while it brings a frown to another. This has bothered every great humorist, who soon learns that, until a joke is tried out on a really large audience, it is not truly "frown-proof." The collective subconscious of an audience decides.

It is the same with tragedy, where the line can be thinly drawn and can bring laughter where it is not intended. Witness the tear-jerking moments in *Uncle Tom's Cabin*—when badly acted by amateurs. Laughter in the wrong place has broken the heart of many a playwright. I remember Maeterlinck telling me about the first production in English of his immortal *Pélleàs and Mélisande*. Mrs. Patrick Campbell was playing the lead, piling up the emotion of this great drama. When Golaud, Mélisande's husband, suspects her of infidelity with his brother, Pélleàs, he loses his temper and beats her mercilessly. Maeterlinck makes Mélisande repeat "Je ne suis pas heureuse," which is a Belgian idiom that means "I am in a terrible situation and don't know what to do!" On the occasion of the London first night attended by Maeterlinck, Mrs. Campbell got absent-minded and uttered "I am not happy," four times instead of three, which brought a convulsion of laughter from the audience.

Laughter at the ludicrous is usually due to a quick drop from great to small. This suddenly builds up an excessive amount of psychic energy which simultaneously constructs a new thought-atmosphere. I noticed this changing state of mind in audiences when my comedy-melodrama *Who's Looney now?* was produced. It was instructive to see how one section swayed with the humor while another merely smiled. My play is based on a true tragedy, the character study of the hero being taken from life.

I wanted to show that someone can become mentally ill and lose his mind, but not his reason. Henry McIntyre, a world famed inventor whose patents and inventions have made him enormously rich, was working on the satellite program when frustrations, caused by Washington authorities, brought on a nervous collapse. His main symptoms manifested themselves on his wedding night when he discovers he has become impotent. He is incarcerated in his own asylum in Santa Barbara, a sea-side resort, where his virgin wife (who he now detests) supervises him by remote control. She finds this fate almost too great a burden to be borne.

Although psychically deranged, much of what her husband says still contains a glitter of truth and at times his mind sparkles like a diamond. His condition represents a disorder of the mind which is not insanity in the strict sense of the word. His wife engages a renowned sexologist from Switzerland who believes that, as soon as his patient's libido is restored, he will recover. The rest of the plot acts out the prescribed remedies, which lead from one tragic-comic situation to another. In a parting piece of advice, McIntyre says to his phoney psychiatrist "You are the type of man who takes himself too seriously. Every once in a while you should go to the mirror and burst out laughing!"

Learning to laugh at ourselves is excellent therapy, especially when people begin to imagine themselves too important, as most of us do now and then. The arguments of my play are, in essence, that in order to understand any situation, be it tragic or happy, one must have been in it oneself and come out of it victoriously. There has to be captivity and then deliverance, if we are to sympathize with any human problem. So how can we judge the deeds of others?

Intuition is possessed in greater amount by women, who are built to receive. A man is obviously physically constructed to expend, and that is why he usually does not last as long as his wife (go to any cemetery and notice the dates of those buried together). The definition of intuition has been put variously but here is a good one from Dr. Robert Kingman: "Information arising suddenly from the subconscious mind, in which is stored a much wider experience, inherited from ancestral memories, than that covered by learned knowledge."

We are all familiar with these emotional intuitions, which usually come with a sudden flash of understanding at the most unlikely times. They come from what experts call "unconscious cerebration," that is to say without any forced mental process. How frequently have we heard the old but wise expression "I feel it in my bones," meaning the intuition is so strong it is almost physiological. Or we say "Speak of the devil!" when a friend appears in person just when he has been in mind or conversation. The subsconscious was aware that this person was due to make an appearance and, for some reason was prompted to announce it to the conscious level.

This type of phenomena is just another manifestation which takes the form of gratituous omens, presentiment, or just plain hunches. They prove over again that the wisest part of our mind is unconscious of itself and that the most rational section may be that which does not reason. Let us, therefore, believe in the fundamental intuitions of the human race which give promptings of future world events to those who know how to "remember" them.

OUT OF THE BODY

The word *psi* was coined to describe psychic energy, about which so little is yet known we can only refer to what it does rather than what it is. We know when we think we use this force. Some think in words, others in pictures. For me, my mind is like a kaleidoscope. The atoms of glass coalesce into thought patterns which fall apart, then reunite. I shake it ever so slightly and the precise combination of my thinking is not likely to be repeated. I cannot liken my mind to a computer, as a modern psychologist might, because my sense of mathematics is non-existent!

Fever is known to favor a phenomenal *psi* experience, especially when it brings on a semi-comatose condition. This can lead, if very rarely, to a fourth-dimensional vision of oneself. The soul seemingly becomes dissociated from the body for a brief period, as if departing. This is a vicarious form of death—the patient "dies" alive, then rallies. Often it is due to life-saving drugs.

Robert Louis Stevenson (1850-1894) lived the last years of his life in the Samoan Islands, beloved by the natives, who called him Chief Tusatala (Teller of Tales). The author of *Dr. Jekyll and Mr. Hyde* consecrated his life to literature. Those who knew him declared that his thought was so clear that it was impossible not to perceive an impression of it even without words uttered. When he voiced it, you seemed less to be hearing him speak than think! He was obviously highly gifted with E.S.P. It is odd to reflect that the primitive people among whom he lived and died in Samoa, understood that he was among the greatest of writers; and that a large part of the literate world did not come to this view until long after he had died.

He suffered from ill-health all his life but he never lived to become senile. The beautiful elasticity of spirit comes through in his letters. They are, in fact, conversation made visible. In person, it is said, his talk was like a fountain falling upon mosses. Here is a psychical experience which he seemed to have understood by a knowledge which defies most people who try to put it into words. It happened when he was suffering a crisis of pulmonary tuberculosis which normally would have been fatal. The local doctor had given him up and his wife was at his side preparing to face bereavement. I paraphrase because the story was told to me by his step-daughter, Mrs. Salisbury Field, whom I knew in Santa Barbara, California. Robert Louis Stevenson himself touched on it in a letter to his friend. F.W.H. Myers, in which he recollected a sense of soul-emancipation.

By ten o'clock on a hot hazy afternoon in 1892, Stevenson was weaker than usual. Respiration was reduced to mere gasps; his heart was throbbing rather than beating and the great writer felt certain that his life was quickly ebbing away.

Suddenly he became aware of a new form of consciousness separate from, and yet not quite superseding, his mortal selfhood in the flesh. Gradually this new consciousness became more individual, as though it were absorbing his past ego—and as it gathered a form of clarity, it seemed to become able to exist outside his body which it could contemplate in full detachment. This new self seemingly could wander at will in whatever direction it wished through space and time.

All the major events of his life were mirrored before him in one great jewel of recollection, a condensation of the memory stream flowing with life through time. At this stage of the experience he had become omnipresent; he was able to get up and leave his body completely. He watched his wife come to his bedside and rush for the doctor. He followed her step by step to the village.

During this interval a loneliness stole over him. A desolate plain loomed before his eyes, low-lying and unlighted, in the center of which there roamed another man whom he did not know. Although he saw and heard all this he could not cry out, as he would have wished. This feeling of gloom ended as

94

he watched the doctor arrive with Mrs. Stevenson. He was comically amused as he saw the man injecting into his arm what he later learned was adrenalin. He smiled as he heard the doctor say: "I am afraid this is the end." In what he called the "divine state of the death-meridian line," he began feeling strange forebodings, alternating with exaltations, in the remnants of his body-bound consciousness—at once grotesque and rapturous. He felt no desire to stir himself, not even to move an eyelid. He was dead.

After what seemed like an eternity his heart began throbbing again with slow intermittent thumps. He was made aware that his mortal consciousness was reviving and drawing back into itself his detached ego. He found it easy to step back into his body, as it were, but in doing so, all the clarity of vision—the unlimited ability to see anything and everything, immediately disappeared.

This experience calls to mind the philosophy of Yoga that embraces the idea the body is a garment to take off and put on at will. Yoga attributes to every human being a sidereal element in which the soul, or spirit, is believed to inhere. In an otherwise dull book, Colonel Sir Alexander Ogston writes in *Reminiscences of Three Campaigns in the South African War,* a truly exciting out-of-the-body experience. I quote from his own words, which make for a better rendition than the case of Stevenson. The Colonel was admitted to the Bloemfontein Hospital in March 1900, suffering from typhoid fever while serving with the forces of Field Marshal Lord Roberts.

"In my delirium," he writes, "night and day made little difference for me. In the four-bedded ward where they first placed me I lay, as it seemed, in a state of stupor, which excluded any hopes or fears. Mind and body appeared to be dual, and to some extent separate. I was conscious of my body as an inert, tumbled mass near the door; of course I knew it belonged to me but it was not I. I was aware that my mental self would often leave my body, always carrying something soft and black, I did not know what, in my left hand. And then it wandered away under grey, sunless, moonless, starless skies, ever onwards to a distant gleam on the horizon—solitary but not unhappy—seeing other dark shades gliding silently by. Then something produced a consciousness that the chilly mass which instinctively I knew was my body, began stirring again. I was then drawn rapidly back to it, joining it with disgust. Mental stability returned as I was fed and cared for.

"I knew that death was hovering about and I remember wondering who and where I would decide to haunt when I became a ghost! I would invariably leave my body after nourishment, wandering off to silent fields, knowing neither light or darkness but roaming on and on beneath murky skies, until the something unknown would draw me back into my body. It always amazed me to see the other patients in the room acting as if my body still contained me.

"As time passed—time for which I had no knowledge as to its duration—these wanderings became more frequent. Always I was summoned back reluctantly to the huddled mass that was my ailing body. On the last occasion, when I was about to reenter, I heard someone say: "He will live!" I sighed and remember finding the pathetic mass of flesh very cold and clammy. All the same, this thing lying near the door and I now grew together again, ceasing to be two separate entities."

Colonel Ogston was bestowed with the fourth-dimensional vision usual in this type of phenomenon. He could see through the walls of stone buildings, in fact all was transparent to his senses. He saw his compatriots fighting to clear the railway line to the Cape, the South African General de Wet giving the British forces no rest. He saw a brother officer in another part of his hospital grow very ill, scream and die. He saw the nurses take his corpse away in shoeless feet so that the other patients would not be upset. This was confirmed later on.

In due course, Sir Alexander rejoined Lord Roberts and when the war ended, he officiated at the peace conference.

THE POWER TO WILL

Have you ever been so annoyed at someone that if your thoughts could kill, the unfortunate soul would have dropped dead? The power to will can be potent both for good and evil. You may have unknowingly more of this power than others and without meaning to do so, may cause havoc or death to others! This happened with Anna Kingsford (1846-1881), a noted Victorian novelist. She knew that she could will things to happen but it never occurred to her that willing could unwittingly be used for killing!

When first married, she and her husband, a prominent anti-vivisectionist, lived in a quiet suburban street near London. She needed quiet for concentration on her writing. Imagine her dismay when each Sunday a barrow man set up his pitch outside her window with his contant cry "Shrimps and watercress," nearly driving Mrs. Kingsford into a state of distraction.

One Sunday, after several of them were spoiled for her work by this irritation, she went into her husband's study and said quite seriously: "I wish someone would choke that man to death!" Then she went outside, took the man's name and reported him to the local police station. She was told nothing could be done.

A few months afterwards, the man's cries were heard no more. The annoyance was forgotten by her busy mind until a few months later, when her husband looked up from his morning paper with a sense of shock. "Anna!" he cried nervously. "Your wish has come true. That barrow-man *is* going to be choked to death! He has been convicted of murdering his wife and has been sentenced to be hanged."

Our willing can be as dangerous as witchcraft if not kept in control. In Africa to this day, there are men who take part in mental duels claiming they can kill their opponents as far away as one hundred miles—just by exercising their psychic energy. At one time these psychic battles were the subject of investigation by the British authorities. No arrow is flown, no spear hurled, yet the person can die.

I mention these outlandish examples to prove the power of thought or will. If negative thinking can destroy, positive thinking must construct. Every thought you create is as real as if it can be seen physically. Your thoughts are continually creating circumstances, especially with your hopes and your fears. Whatever the mind keeps uppermost is likely to come to pass, be it bad or good. Any constant thinking or imagining is capable of forming itself into a reality—because thoughts are an unseen magnet for coming events.

Willing positively for good health has been proven by those who practice it; there is simply no denying its power. It is a practical demonstration in their personal histories and speaks for itself. Of course, there are exceptions where willing is stymied, such as with incurable diseases, terrible bodily accidents, or other personal disasters, but people who have suffered them and adopted the positive thought-atmosphere, have left the world richer by facing tragedy as it should be faced. They refused to let it become proud.

The healing power, within which some are certainly gifted, is merely a system of willing for others—through divine meditation. The secret is that the invalid must be in complete sympathy and must abandon any doubts for the cure, and because this cooperation is lacking, the system has its failures.

The power to will for positivity should be a compound of constancy, firmness, and perseverance. In this way, you charge your thought-currents. Every day you can think yourself into a finer facial expression. If your thoughts are permanently cheerful and constructive, your face will look younger and firmer.

To allow oneself to be affected by the ill-will or even the indifference of others, is a weakness many of us have. It is always sad to be misunderstood or ill-judged. In escaping into the psychic world every person must be his or her own explorer and discoverer and must not be perturbed if the treasures found are scoffed at by others. We all have to put up with the malignity of the world at large, which is made up of civilized parrots. They think they know everything, but they are utterly without a standard with which they can measure themselves spiritually. They think they are clever because they have discovered they have the power of killing truths by other truths. Don't try to argue with them when they attack your ideas.

Just send out daily and healing thoughts to those who may be in need of them, using the great power of sympathy with which you have been endowed. We should telegraph these thoughts with all the psychic energy we can muster in our E.S.P. apparatus. Leave it to the recipients to translate them into mental peace and wholesomeness. It will not only help them but it will test your powers of willing.

A PHANTOM COMPANION

In Tibet man is in continual conflict with the elements; he is faced by mountains that brook no crossing; the earth gives little or no food; snow, ice, hail, and burning sun smite his crops; and it is little wonder that implacable demons and fiends seem ever to be seeking his destruction and mock him from the distant snows.

Madame David-Neel, a diminutive, Parisian-born explorer, was the first white woman to enter the Forbidden City of Lhasa and knows a side of Tibetan life which is a sealed book to most explorers. She has spent years in the Land of Eternal Snows, is the friend of hermits who sit for years in mountain caves in the vow of darkness and silence, and has witnessed many of the weird ceremonies for which Tibet is famous.

An example of these is "chod," a mystic banquet and ceremony of initiation for those who want to become lamas. The site chosen is usually a wild, lonely place calculated to increase the eeriness of the proceedings, and the hour is always at dusk.

"A little ballet is performed by ascetics in ritual robes wearing horrible masks," explains Madame David-Neel in one of her books. "These initiates become so stimulated in their imagination that they actually believe they are preparing themselves to be devoured by demons.

"The celebrant must concentrate on a feminine deity that stands before him with a bloody sword in her emaciated hands and in one fell swoop cuts off the heads of the dancers. Cohorts of ghouls then crowd near for the feast. The goddess severs their limbs, opens up their bellies and devours them.

"When the mental torture has become unbearable, the novice is permitted to let the demonic vision of the banquet vanish. Gradually the hideous laughter of the ghouls fades away and the initiate must imagine that he himself has become a mass of charred bones."

The climax of Madame David-Neel's Tibetan career was reached when she learned to create actual material forms in the image of her thought by sheer power of concentration. The pert little Frenchwoman had become lonely in the solitude of a mountain retreat and she decided to carry out the secret formula, for she knew that a successful thought-form appears to its creator, as well as to others, as an objective human being.

"I chose for my experiment," she told one of her friends, "a most insignificant character—a man that would be quite safe—short and fat, of an innocent and jolly type." And verily, after a few months, Madame David-Neel's man was finished, his bulky figure growing gradually life-like and usable.

"For a time he did various chores for me but then I found him doing things that I did not command. He would stop and look around when I was undressing. I would sometimes feel his robe brushing against me."

Then an awful thing happened. The man began to alter. Before her very eyes he slowly changed into a lean and evil-looking fellow.

On one occasion a herdsman delivering milk saw the phantom and took immediate flight, informing the district about his experience so that the little woman and her phantom companion became totally isolated.

It took Madame David-Neel about six months to dissolve the man with the help of the formula the hermits had taught her, so tenacious of life was he.

THE FACES ON THE CATHEDRAL WALL

Damp within a wall has a way of sometimes manifesting itself in the form of peculiar stains, either because of increasing dampness or the drying out of internal moisture.

Several such stains appeared some time ago in the south aisle of Christchurch Cathedral in Oxford. Eventually it was noticed that they had begun taking on the lineaments of human faces.

Under the Burne-Jones window, donated by the late Dean Liddells in memory of his daughter and son-in-law (the world-renowned artist), there appeared the profile of an elderly man with a crown of curly white hair and an acquiline nose.

Upon closer examination it was found that another face had begun to form, apparently that of a woman, at considerable height in another part of the aisle.

In about a month the features of the first face had matured sufficiently so that it could be identified as the face of Dean Henry George Liddells himself whose grave was only a few yards away in the Close outside. He was buried there in 1898.

The other face turned out to be a famous chorister whose voice had rung through the great edifice for many years. Her grave also was not far away.

Strangely enough the wall where these manifestations took place had taken on a blueish-white appearance, quite distinct from the usual discoloration in other parts of the Cathedral.

Scientists and psychical research experts have examined the faces, and the former have declared that the composition of the stone is not of a type liable to undergo chemical change. They have also satisfied themselves that the portraits have not been embroidered from obscure markings by human hands. Due to public curiosity the Cathedral authorities have conveniently hidden the faces, one by a new altar and the other by a large board.

The explanation proposed by an official of the British Psychical Research Society assumes that the emotional part of the earthly memories of a man of great gifts would naturally linger round the spot where he took pains to erect a memorial to his daughter, and especially amid surroundings he loved.

The Dean having been a great speaker and the chorister a great singer, that is, the personalities of both having been accustomed to pervading the building in the form of dynamic sound, the effects of their presence would last longer than those of others. It is interesting to note that the Dean's expression, formerly one of austerity, has been replaced by gentleness and benignity.

A similar manifestation was reported many years before this in the South Wales *Echo and Evening Express* for October, 1898, in which the face of Dean Vaughan, once attached to the staff of Llandaff Cathedral, formed from a stain that appeared on the left-hand side of the main entrance. The stain appeared shortly after the Dean's death and grew steadily until it had produced a striking likeness. Authorities declared that they were convinced no human agency was responsible, and the stain eventually dried back as mysteriously as it had formed. It remains to be seen whether the face of Dean Liddells will do the same.

SECTION FOUR

OUR ETERNITY

The hypothesis of reincarnation must be examined in any treatise which attempts to discuss parapsychological events in relation to psychic realities. Why has this hypothesis played so small a part in the religious psychology of the Western World? Its main premise—that after we die, the psychic composition of our egos, intuitions, instincts, and dreams, take up their abode in another earthly body in order to reconciliate themselves with destiny—satisfies the mind and heart and soul among millions of Orientals and Asians. Westerners are among a small minority who do not believe in reincarnation but is not the very idea of immortality a suggestion of it?

If you think about it, who else could have lived your life with all its difficulties and triumphs, except yourself? There is an impressive galaxy of great names who felt this way and believed themselves to have been reincarnations—from Goethe, Walt Whitman, Victor Hugo, Jack London to Napoleon, Frederick the Great, General George Patton, and (still living out his incarnation), Dr. Norman Vincent Peale.

How else explain the way so many great composers have exhibited their gifts before they were able to toddle, or how Yehudi Menuhin was able to play perfectly on a miniature violin at the age of three? (In the words of Fritz Kreisler, he never had the pleasure of mastering his art.) Is it possible that these child prodigies, in all walks of talent, are those who excelled in former lives and were not given enough time to

103

complete their mission?

Today, Dr. Ian Stevenson, a respected psychiatrist at the University of Virginia, is running what he calls a Laboratory for the Investigation of Suggestive Cases of Reincarnation. He claims to have found a great many such cases, some of which he feels are support for the hypothesis. Dr. Stevenson has also discovered, living in an Eastern part of Alaska, about ten thousand Indians (not Eskimos), who have been practicing a religion which includes beliefs in the theory of rebirth, for hundreds of years. These people believe that they start life again where it left off last time.

Mistakenly some object to reincarnation because they feel it is based on punishment. They misunderstand the idea of karma, which is retributive justice for wrong-doing in the past life—but reward for goodness, too. Karma means we are born superior or inferior babies with certain debts which must be paid. This law states that for every action there must be a reaction. Excess of suffering comes to those with larger karmic debts, which simply means they have to work harder to pay them off as soon and as willingly as possible—and the suffering ceases.

This, for me, explains the many injustices and benefits of humanity. Our lives can be summed up as variations of an eternal theme—we are reborn to feel, to hope, to love, to suffer, to weep and to die—and to be reborn again. It could be compared to the foundation of the perfect state—a partnership between those still living, those who are "dead," and those yet to be born. Just as all of nature hands on its reborn forms and patterns, so the human soul inherits itself.

A few years ago I read about Dr. Wilder Penfield, of the Montreal Neurological Institute, discovering an area in the cerebral cortex of the human brain which, when lightly stimulated by electrodes, would touch off memory regression. Patients thus treated would relive episodes of their remote childhood and sometimes of a past life they remembered. The recall was so very realistic it compared to a tape recording of past events, and strangest of all, these patients were aware their memories were working. Such is not the case with hypnosis. Memory regression into past lives using hypnosis which blots out all consciousness has had dubious results.

Perhaps the time will soon be at hand when electronic stimulation to certain brain centers will bring out the past incarnation of an interested person. It may be in this convolution of the cortex neurologists will find the still secret records of preexistence.

Interestingly, this subject itself is continually being reincarnated in popularity. Every few decades there is a new surge of enthusiasm from the public, a recent example being Bernstein's *Search for Bridie Murphy*. Back in 1915, an American national magazine published a series of convincing cases. In one of the most compelling a commercial photographer named Ethel Byrne and living in Albany, New York, told of her half-sister, Ketty, who was fifteen years her junior. Miss Byrne was often in charge of the baby and was struck by her manners, which seemed to belong to bygone days. At the age of two, she seemed to be acting from habit rather than from parental tutoring. There was further suggestion in the way she would utter casually pieces of recondite information, which she had no possible way of knowing. This worried and also confounded the household.

As soon as she was able to talk articulately, Ketty hinted that she had lived before. She would be overheard telling herself about a fey world, peopled by trolls, elves, and other supernatural beings. When reproved, she once threatened she would leave. Asked where she would go, she replied curtly "Back to heaven, of course. Where else?"

A couple of years passed and Miss Byrne found Ketty increasingly insistent that she had been here before. Questioned, her tiny voice would trumpet "Oh, I've been here many times before, sometimes as a girl but also as a boy." On a later occasion she declared "I lived in Canada in one of my lives. I was a soldier then and I fought in the war. I took the gates!"

She then gave the name of Captain Lishus Faber, an improbable name for an English soldier and his taking the gates just didn't make much sense. The family felt Ketty should be discouraged, so when she mooted past lives, they shut her up. By the first signs of her womanhood, they were all pleased she had forgotten the psychic nonsense which had been deluding her.

Then an incurable disease laid its terrible hands upon her and she died. Before she expired, the child asked for a mirror. Taking it to reflect her poor emaciated little face, she was not shocked. "This body is like one of my party dresses. It is now worn out and I shall be given a new body in its place. This one was made especially for my life here, but now I shall have a beautiful new one, like Ethel's new dress."

Long afterwards, Ethel was friendly with a history professor from the university in Albany. It was in the winter of 1911 and one day, during table-talk over a cup of coffee, she mentioned to him the weird case of her deceased sister. The professor became very interested and researched the ordnance records of Canada at the time of the Indian wars. First he discovered that there was such a commonly used phrase "take the gates," which meant to be in charge of a strategic fortification.

Encouraged, he delved through the records back to the year 1660, finding a Captain Alonysius Febre who was assigned to "take the gates" at the Battle for Montreal. He was with the Marquis de Tracy in the once-famous Carignan-Salieres Regiment. The Captain had distinguished himself in the victory for the French, which broke the power of the Iroquois Indians. The similarity between Ketty's referral to Lishus Faber spoke for itself.

If this case stood alone, there might be some excuse for doubt, but it does not. There are many similar cases of children, fated to die young, whose evidence is unsophisticated and unencumbered by education. There is the touching story of Shanti Devi, which I published in my book *Who's There?*, about an Indian child whose family believed in reincarnation, as all devout Hindus do. Shanti Devi remembered her former incarnation so vividly that, at the age of four, she located the husband of a past life, now forty years old!

Preexistence, strictly speaking, involves the transmigration of souls as Pythagorus argued but some cases defy being categorized. One which came to my notice began as a series of dreams experienced by a young English boy who later became a distinguished barrister in England, a member of the Inner Temple. His name was Frank Grisewood and he died aged 70 in 1968.

During his pre-adolescent period, Frank was with his parents on a two week holiday from school. In all his dreams at that time, he found himself living in a fine old English country mansion, during what appeared to be the period of Charles I. The details of the house and surrounding country-side made a deep impression and he recalled them in detail.

The main character of these dreams was a member of the mansion's domestic staff, a trooper who gave the name of Jan Persefoot. Frank's parents listened to their son tell anecdotes of this man, whose antics outdid those of John Gilpin and the benevolent Dick Whittingdon. Jan would tell Frank of other stately mansions where he had lived, with fantastic pleasure gardens and flanking copses bordering a winding river.

At first his parents saw no reason to discourage Frank in his nocturnal excursions, but soon they began to fear he might be forming a neurotic attachment to his dream life. The child would tell of long rides with Jan, pacing him on a shaggy pony. One morning Mrs. Grisewood found Frankie shading his eyes while still asleep, as if dazzled by bright lights. When he awoke he told his mother that the gleam of the sun on Jan's helmet had given him a headache. He said he had been talking to his friend from a bedroom window in the castle. In that particular chat, Jan expounded his philosophy on women, whom he described as "amiable emollients of our life, an ointment necessary for us in manhood . . ."

The Grisewoods could not understand how their son had ever heard of such salutations used by Jan as "my little gamepoult," and "my lambkin," which were Medieval expressions. They attributed them to familiarity with some older boy's history book at school. Among his many adventures,

Jan told Frankie of being captured by pirates and chained naked to a galley. Another was about a trip to the Low Countries where, to save himself from an enemy, Jan was forced to cut the dykes and flood the countryside for miles around.

Then came a dream where Jan said goodbye to Frankie and his parents were relieved. This last dream happened a couple of nights before the lad returned to boarding school. He woke up crying profusely, reporting that Jan had said: "Don't be too good or too bad, my young gamepoult. And may God bless you as he has myself!" Waving his hand in farewell, he rode off, whistling a tune Frankie could not remember.

Seven years passed and Frank Grisewood, now nineteen and an under-graduate at Oxford, was invited to stay with his roommate in a Northamptonshire home. He had never been there before, and as the motor car drew up in front of a Jacobean mansion, built in the early Seventeenth Century, Frankie was brought up short with a *déjà vu* shock. As he described it later to a reporter: "I just gasped. It was unquestionably the old castle I knew in my dreams. Much of the woodland had been cleared away but the house was exactly as I remembered it."

Once inside, he made his way, as if somnabulistically, almost neglecting to greet his hosts, into the great hall. "They have taken away the tapestry there!" he exclaimed. "There used to be a window on that side. It must have been bricked up."

Naturally enough his hosts were nonplussed. "Can it be you have lived here before? How do you know so much about our home?"

"In a sense I did live here before. Let me find my way about and I will tell you more."

Upstairs and along winding passages he went until he came to an ante-chamber overlooking the main greensward in front. Automatically he tapped the wall of this small bedroom and it echoed hollow. Further examination proved there had once been a window which was now blocked up, perhaps due to the "window tax" period.

"I used to wave to Jan Persefoot from this window," he told his friends as he unwound the mystery of his dream series. "There's the stream where he taught me to catch trout!" And during the course of that weekend he was able to tell his new hosts many facts which they did not know about the old home which they had bought thirty years earlier, and where Frank had lived several hundred years ago.

* * * *

While these two true stories do not illustrate karmic truths, which involve a system of credits and debits, they stress the way the philosophy can give courage to the weak and hearten the disheartened. Karmic debts can be paid by kindness to others and then forgotten. You either pay as you go or pay in another life!

THE LIGHT BEYOND

When I was a lad in London I remember seeing an exhibit in a museum which started me thinking along the lines of the subject for this book. It was a human body chemically reduced to its original elements. They were tied up in packages, or capped in bottles, carefully labeled. I noted so many gallons of water, the same that falls from rain; there was some sodium chloride, the same that we use on food as salt; and of course there were all the metals and minerals, such as carbonate of lime, iron, and phosphates.

Needless to say, I was disgusted, for this was not my idea of myself in spite of the fact all my component elements known to the chemist was present—minus one. The chemical engineer has never, nor ever will, bring down the spiritual part of man to a chemical formula. Even Darwin was unable to say what it is that evolutes in the human being. It is of course the spiritual part of him. The body terrestrial is different from the body celestial. Then why could not this exhibit have foot-noted that the human spirit contains the unseen correspondences of the exhibited ingredients, much finer and more subtle? In one word, our immortal soul.

Sooner or later most people are faced with a bereavement so painful it changes their patterned concept of reality and even their attitude toward life itself. Where do our departed loved ones go? That is a question which has preoccupied many fine minds, including Albert Einstein. Before he died, he spoke of a "Beyond" in one of his scientific books, a part of the Universe which will never be sighted by man no matter how far space exploration advances. Due to the peculiarities of light in a gravitational field, he predicted this haven would always be beyond man's knowledge. Can this be where those we love foregather?

Other great men, who have become world-famous, have found solace in their bereavements through spiritualism, which can banish sorrow, and they firmly believed that the human personality does survive the shock of death. There is quite a galaxy of names since Sir Oliver Lodge started a very dynamic movement in England. Inspired by the belief that spiritualism is an experience of truth, he was able to investigate its philosophy in relation to physics.

Another systematic thinker, Sir William Crookes (1832-1919), also a great physicist, who gave the world the Crookes lens and whose inventions in this field helped to bring to perfection the television screen, lost his wife prematurely and joined a spiritualist circle late in the last century. Instead of his wife materializing a beautiful young woman appeared within the ectoplasm. She said her name was Katie King, that she was the daughter of a notorious English pirate! She told Sir William that she had died a young woman about two hundred years before he met her. He met her on several occasions at other seances and finally he fell in love with her. Gossip said that he had gone through a form of marriage with her, but this was never confirmed.

Regardless of what denigration is brought against spiritualism, it once built a university! When Governor Leland Stanford was California's ruler, he and his wife lost their only son, aged sixteen. They sorrowed unspeakably until a friend took them to a seance. The "dead" son appeared and asked his father and mother to build an institution of higher learning in his name. So Leland Stanford Jr. University was created, still standing today near San Francisco.

Then there was the case of a prime minister who governed Canada with advice from the spirit world. William Lyon MacKenzie King (1874-1950) never married. When his mother died, he found that he could receive messages from her which helped him greatly in his private life. Then, after becoming Prime Minister of Canada—elected for several terms—he was able to communicate with some of the important statesmen of the past, such as Prime Ministers Balfour and Gladstone of England whose advice helped him steer Canada through the critical years of World War Two.

The list of other believers is a very long one and includes such thinkers as Goethe, Mark Twain, Maeterlinck, Walt Whitman, Sir Arthur Conan Doyle, the Nobel Prize-winning French physicist, Charles Richet, Air Chief Marshal Lord Dowding (Chief of the Fighter Command in the Battle of Britain)—to name only a few.

I may say that I am not a spiritualist but I do believe in the possibility of communication with the dead as a result of my personal philosophic contemplation of the sensory universe. I confess the physical signs of survival for the human personality are not necessary to me because I feel it is true without this proof. I do not feel I need to sit in the dark with a medium who will show me the dead are still alive. Nor do I need to hear their voices through a trumpet to be absolutely sure it is the spirit he or she claims to be. For me a life gone from sight and hearing certainly is not lost.

Fraudulent mediums have besmirched a cult which tries to be genuinely religious. I can vouch that the majority of mediums are honest souls—however much they are accused by doubters that they deceive themselves and others who employ them. I can well imagine that those who have been privileged to see the face of a loved one at a seance find it unforgettable. The psychical experience of "feeling" the presence of a departed mother or father can be just as subjective and as valuable to the participant as life itself.

I am sure that some of my readers have come close, now and then, to this phenomenon. Some might be inclined to deny its psychic nature, if questioned, but such experiences are, I am convinced, far less rare than is supposed. The books of Stewart Edward White (1873-1946) were proof-positive for masses of interested readers that this is true and, for a while, inhibitions about discussing these events were disregarded.

He was first known as a highly successful writer of adventure stories, a Western writer (not just a writer of "Westerns"). He and his wife, Betty, became spiritualists and their books on the subject were very widely read. One, a best-seller, "The Unobstructed Universe," was a detailed account of posthumous communications with his departed wife, Elizabeth Grant White, which explores places far more adventurous than any Stewart had created in his novels.

I knew the Whites when they lived in Santa Barbara. He was courteous but rather shy, while Betty had the quality of making everyone feel at home in her company. Her face was remarkable, not only for its type of special beauty, but for its innocence, eagerness and gaiety. She discovered her mediumship quite by accident. One day, when she and a friend were in a large San Francisco department store, they purchased a Ouija Board. Agog with curiosity, she and her husband amused themselves that night for an hour as the needle-pointer spelled out various commonplace messages. Then without warning, the indicator began rushing over the alphabetical board so rapidly they had some difficulty in following its composition of words.

When transcribed, it turned out to be a message from Betty's mother, who had died when she was an infant. The "dead" woman made her identity very clear (and spirits always go to great lengths to do this), informing Betty that she would use her exclusively as her medium. Not only did her mother continue to live with her as if she had never died, Betty too continued to live with her husband after she had physically vanished.

After further experiments with the Ouija Board, the

Whites took to automatic writing and found it a more satisfactory method of communication. In this the recipient hears no voices, sees no spirit figures. Betty's procedure was to pass into trance, her forehead resting on her palm, a pencil in her right hand which she allowed to travel rapidly across a large sheet of paper—transcribing messages from her spirit-mother. This entity in turn sent messages from other spirits.

The automatic writer usually has no knowledge of what is being written through the pencil and even after perusing the meanderings on the sheets of paper afterwards, often displays surprise at the text. Betty White turned out to be very endowed in this form of interplay with the cosmos, which many possess and are not aware of. She found she could use its consummate power, but just as her mother was about to delve into interesting secrets about life in the hereafter, communication suddenly ceased. Mr. and Mrs. White were left with a feeling of rejection.

One evening some months later, Betty was feeling queasy and, while lying down, fell into a state of semi-consciousness. Her speech became halting and her ears began to ring with sentences seemingly uttered at random. It was recalled later that she felt it was rather like listening to an old radio which spluttered and whistled. Finally the words came clearly. She was able to moan into speech those that came by mental impression or through the "inner ear." All of this her husband laboriously put down on paper. It was evident that Betty had been invaded by a new etheric personality. Somewhat later, still another of these personalities supervened. It was made manifest by Betty's voice changing to an entirely new timbre when in trance.

In White's last book, *With Folded Wings,* published one year before his death, White explored, with the help of his spirit guides, what death does to personality: "It is a further journey which gives you greater and simpler opportunities for development. The mechanism which you carry from this life has been built for a life beyond. If you have not accomplished much constructive work here, you will approach your future opportunities a little crippled. But you will be given the ability to heal this defect by appropriate effort."

He wonders why Christians pray against sudden death for he felt a quick end is the best. He quotes an invisible informant: "The normal end of life on earth is a ripening, by which the forces are withdrawn into the seed naturally and easily. Many, however, are fated to be struck down by accidents or untoward chance before the sap of earth has ceased to flow. The real orientation is toward transition into the beyond ... Death is usually gentle. Never worry about dying..." And when his own turn came to die, White faced it as had his beloved Betty, not just with serenity but with eagerness and joy.

What we call death, then, is merely the divestment of an outer shell from the spirit, which can use it no more. Maurice Maeterlinck whose early plays dramatized the tyranny of death, felt that life, as we know it here, is only the first act of an eternal drama, the end of a terrestrial existence—merely a pause. Indeed, life itself is the best argument against death because all that is life has an insistent urge to survive. If the human soul did not inherit itself, it would have to be against the great dictums of nature.

Maeterlinck, a giant of the intellect, did not believe everyone survives the shock of death. Those that do, whose psychic energy surpasses that barrier, he was convinced are capable of communication. Here he is with his thoughts on survival in a hitherto unpublished piece we wrote together: "We must not lose hope. There is incontestably a Beyond of which we know nothing. What does seem strange is that the discarnated personalities never touch on subjects we would wish. Would it not be wonderful to learn that the religion in which they died is the true one, that all its warning and rewards are real?

"Whenever the dead come into our minds, it is altogether probable that they are trying to attract our attention. If they were assured that we hear them stirring within us in this way, perhaps they would be encouraged to help us more than they do. It is the final tragedy of death when spirits try to speak to the living and receive no answer. Spiritualists believe that they speak to the dead, but there always seem to be difficulties on both sides which make so many of these communications unsatisfactory. Might it be a question of wavelengths? The day is coming when we shall know much more about the behavior of thought-waves in the immaterial universe."

William Butler Yeats, another Nobel Prize-winner, felt sure that the human personality persists in an after-life. He held séances at the Old Abbey Theater in Dublin, which was built over the former city morgue. These séances were especially successful and evidential and he was led finally to write a brilliant spiritualistic one-act play called *The Words upon the Window-pane.* The setting is at Celbridge, where Jonathan Swift often visited Venessa (Esther Vanhomrigh) at her home there, near Dublin. Her jealousy over his friendship with Stella (Esther Johnson) hastened her premature death. The passion of these two women for this extraordinary man is one of the unsolved love triangles of literary history.

In 1723 Vanessa took the desperate step of writing to Stella, pleading with her to give Swift up. Swift rode over to Celbridge afterwards, petrified her with a frown, and flung the letter she had written into her face. Venessa was dead in three weeks, leaving behind a few lines of a poem Swift had written to her, scratched upon her window. In this room Yeats sets his fine play: Members of a Dublin spiritualist group have come to hold a séance. And in short order, the spirit personalities of Vanessa, Stella, plus Jonathan Swift, come through the mouth of the medium and argue out their own versions of what is considered to have been a love affair that ruined the lives of all concerned.

That there are mandatories in the Beyond, who guide or suggest to the living, was admitted by the Archbishop of Canterbury's Committee on Spiritualism in 1950: "We think it probable that the hypothesis that communications proceed in some cases from discarnate spirits is a true one. There is no reason why we should not accept gladly the assurance that we are still in the closest contact with those who were dear to us in this life."

The report winds up, in a rather tortured sentence: "If Spiritualism, with all its aberrations aside, and with every care taken to present it humbly and accurately, contains a truth, it is important to see that truth, not as a new religion but only as filling up certain gaps in our knowledge, so that where we already walk by faith, we may now have some measure by sight as well."

MAETERLINCK'S SEARCH FOR PHENOMENA

"We have to live in the sublime. Where else can we live?" asks Maurice Maeterlinck in one of his essays. One might add to that and say the eternal life is not necessarily the future one—it is merely one in harmony with the true order of values. In this sense, Maeterlinck became an explorer of the world about him. He was the first writer to discover that truth is an abstract and can only be understood by the abstract use of the imagination. For this reason he has often been described as a fourth dimensional writer.

This Nobel Prize-winning literary laureate, who died in 1949, was himself a phenomenon. He was born in a non-literary middle-class Belgium family, who felt his chosen vocation of writing had ruined them socially! The remarkable achievements of his books and plays cannot be explained in purely human terms. Nor can analysis of his natural gifts lay bare the secret of his literary powers. He was unique, and he has enriched literature with a fresh idiom of psychic relationships. No other great writer has made better use of psychic phenomena in his works.

Since his youth, Maeterlinck was urged by an inner drive for proof of survival of the human personality. He was one of the founders of the Psychical Research Society in France. Once he said to me "I believe that my most important work will begin some time after I die."

All his ideas are worth considering. He felt that death is like an anaesthetic, from which some awake sooner than others. He believed there is an enormous fund of knowledge

116

in the etheric atmosphere with which he had been able to tune in for the benefit of his writing. The subject of clairvoyance fascinated him so much he wrote a play, using it as a theme. It is still performed and is called *Interior*, a one-act masterpiece, which brilliantly explores the mystery of a telepathic vision.

The Blue Bird play is a crisp treatment of the fairy tale about two children who are dreaming the same dream. In this he develops his theory that life is a dream which is dreaming another dream—that our waking life is actually an extension of the dream state. This poses the question, of course: Are we more intelligent asleep than when awake?

Although Maeterlinck's ideas are complicated, his style is so simple one has the feeling of understanding them thoroughly. He was able to clothe unfathomable thoughts and shadowy images in a language which appeals to the average reader, hence his enormous public. As a boy he knew he possessed an extension of vision. It was to him like a talent for music is to others. Some are born with it, some not. With the help of Mellarmé, Verhaeren, and Huysmans, he founded the Symbolist movement, aimed at bringing to poetry a faculty of hinting at feelings rather than stating them. Often he would use this device in his plays, as in the superbly dramatic death scene in *Pélleàs and Mélisande*, accompanied by De Bussy's majestically mournful music.

Other world-famed composers, such as Rachmaninoff, Schoenberg, Gabriel Fauré, Chausson, Sibelius, Paul Dukas, and a long list of others lesser known, have been attracted to his librettos because they offer a psychical expression of moods, particularly of longing and regret. Many of the plots of his plays steer dexterously between this world and the next.

Maeterlinck went through three distinct creative periods. First he wrote a series of pessimistic plays, such as *Pélleàs*, mainly about the tyranny of death over life. Some time later, when he fell in love with Georgette Le Blanc, a celebrated French actress-singer, this event stimulated his literary output and he wrote *The Blue Bird* plus its sequel, *The Betrothal*. In this period he was writing about the power of life over death—immortality. In these plays he used his psychic vision.

We once discussed *Mona Vanna,* which involves a war of the Italian Renaissance, and served as a starring vehicle for Sarah Bernhardt and later for Elenora Duse. The plot begins with the conqueror of Pisa demanding, as terms for peace, that Mona Vanna, daughter of the Governor of Pisa and the wife of the military commander, be sent to his tent "naked under her mantle." The beauty of Mona is acclaimed far and wide, hence she is a prize. Since no other way the city of Pisa can be saved, she, her father, and her husband agree to the terms.

I said to Maeterlinck that, for me, it was out of character for them all to agree, that there should have been dissent of, at least, her father. Immediately he retorted "There you are quite wrong because I saw Mona Vanna present herself to the conqueror thus attired." In other words she carried out this act by her own volition in his mind. For Maeterlinck this was reality.

He told me he would create the characters for his plays in the special chamber of his mind, then let them clash with each other as personalities—and they would dictate the play to him. Sometimes mediums were used by him. He visited one in Paris when he was stymied with the plot of a play. She went into trance and without any prompting by him, placed the situation accurately which had brought him to the impasse. But she was unable to help further and he was forced to return to his own methods.

A play called *The Death of Tintagiles* was created about this time from a plot which came to him during a nightmare. It has been produced all over the world and was acted by Judith Anderson when young. It is the story of a beautiful boy child who has incurred the displeasure of an omnipotent queen of a mythical land. He has been condemned to death by suffocation at the hands of the queen herself. All the night terrors of children are depicted in this supernatural story—with the mounting sensation of distress, the indefinite feeling of utter helplessness. These, as well as allied psychical conditions, are all subtly documented, with the play ending on muffled screams.

The third and last period of Maeterlinck's creative life was ushered in by another love affair. At the age of sixty, an astonished public learned that he had married Renée Dahon, an eighteen-year-old actress, ending his twenty year association with Georgette Le Blanc. Instead of writing plays about romance, as his public hoped, the great writer turned to entomology. He wrote his immortal *Life of the Bee,* and the lives of various species of ants.

As his life was drawing to its close, he wrote some books about psychic phenomena. *Before the Great Silence,* and *The Great Beyond,* came from his pen. Earlier he wrote *The Unknown Guest*—an exhaustive study of the psychic world. No facet of the supernormal escaped him—faith healing, stigmatization, water-dowsing, poltergeist activity, even the superstituion of the evil eye. This book did a great service to the then young science of psychical research, and established investigators welcomed him to their ranks.

On the other hand, since he was born a Roman Catholic, the book was condemned by the Church and his name added to the list of banned books by the Index Prohibitorium—with the single exception of his play, *The Blue Bird.*

In summing up his views, he concludes there are obviously unknown natural laws which one day will be postulated and proved and will form the basis for a new branch of knowledge. This is currently happening fifty years later!

"Do we know what it is that dies in the dead?" he once asked me. "Psychic energy definitely can continue after the tomb, and we shall one day understand much more about this great force. I suspect that what it is that dies is recycled in one way or another. The word death will ultimately become obsolete as it has in certain primitive languages, where the word is substituted for *vanish* or the like."

For a mind such as Maeterlinck's, the world of spirits lay open to him like a world of real people. In seeing his supernatural plays, one knows that if spirits exist, they would speak and act as he makes them. He does not try to propound theories of explanations for the mysteries he examines. It is perhaps because he felt more than other writers, their vast mysteriousness.

His works have an immense range. He wrote books about stars, the life in space, higher mathematics, reincarnation, the life of plants and flowers, ancient Egypt, pigeons and spiders, the subconscious, also a long series of essays on mysticism—even a play about chromosomes. In all these we are confronted with stupendous mysteries which are brilliantly described but not elucidated. They are stated poignantly to our emotions and our imaginations, reflecting the universal knowledge he possessed.

In short, Maeterlinck truly lived in two worlds: one was limited, practical, and positive; the other a world that opened into two infinities, one of thought and one of soul. His great gift was in exploring the vaults and corridors of the human soul.

In his plays he seems to be saying we cannot master fate but we can study its secrets and learn to know ourselves the better in the process. *The Blue Bird* sounds an alarm to which we should harken—that the human spirit has need of nature and is itself threatened by anything seeking to destroy what is natural. From any angle we study his works, which are prisms of life here or in the hereafter, Maeterlinck's message seems to be: May a word to the wise be sufficient.

In his power of spiritual flight, he writes about the highest altitudes, often above the level of human thinking—but from there he brings down sun-lighted truths which glow with the radiance of that rarified ethos. He does not insist that a spirit world is the answer to death, but he stresses over and over again that no one is ever really dead until they are forgotten.

As a man he was an idealist of the purest temper, reverencing, with delight, the spiritual riches he found in human nature. In person he was the possessor of a majesty of manner, yet humble and self-effacing. Widely acknowledged as he was for his art, we who were close to him are apt to think less of this, during moments of recollection, than the fact he was the most unselfish and lovable of human beings.

A FORGOTTEN AMERICAN SEERESS

Since Abraham Lincoln died, evidence that he dabbled in Spiritualism has piled up. Among the many papers left by Sir Oliver Lodge to the Society for Psychical Research, was a letter from Dr. Ridgeley Martin, a friend of President Lincoln's, who lived in North Baltimore, Ohio. The letter, dated December 1926, was written to a Mr. W.R. Bradbrook in England about the death of Lincoln's son, Robert Todd Lincoln.

It refers to a séance Dr. Martin had attended in the White House with the President. During this séance, the mother of Lincoln came through with evidential effect, and also Anne Rutledge, his alleged sweetheart (whose closeness to him is now discredited by historians). In passing, we might also refer to Sir Arthur Conan Doyle's claim that he had found evidence pointing to a séance being responsible for the Emancipation Proclamation in 1862.

The séance to which Dr. Martin referred was early in 1865, at about the time Lincoln was posing for the statue which now stands in the Rotunda of the Capitol. This was executed by a beauteous seventeen-year-old girl named Vinnie Ream (1847-1914) who also sculpted the statue of Admiral Farragut in Farragut Square.

This little lady flits across the stage of history in an intensely dramatic role. Not only did she create a life-size image of Lincoln with a penetrating insight into his greatness, but also she was responsible—to some extent at least—for saving the man he had chosen to succeed him in emergency, from an impeachment conviction. It is a fascinating story with some interesting psychic overtones.

Vinnie Ream, later Mrs. Hoxie, won a national competition to do Lincoln's statue, being chosen from many other contestants. A studio was set up for her in the basement of the White House. Lincoln gave her only five sittings out of his busy schedule. During that time he became so enchanted with her winsome personality and beauty that his wife became quite unpleasant to Miss Ream. In those few half hours, Lincoln discussed some of his problems with Vinnie. He explained how he wished to show magnanimity toward the South, bringing about reconstruction rather than psychological destruction. He prayed he would last long enough to do so, but he confided his doubts. He mentioned to her a dream which was foreboding for his future. (As the world knows, he later dreamed all the details of his forthcoming assassination and wrote them down in all their premonitory horror.)

After he was murdered, Vinnie went on chipping away in her small studio until she became the subject of the venom of the Republican cabal, which was opposed to Lincoln's generous attitude toward the South. Captivated by Lincoln during those few sittings, Vinnie was determined to make the statue a masterpiece. Doubtless she was too vocal with her admiration for one day she was informed that her studio was closed and further work on the sculpture must be suspended. Innocent of any intrigue herself, she was now the victim of political hatred.

When he inherited the office from Lincoln, President Andrew Johnson was anxious to follow as closely as he could with his great predecessor's ideas. He soon collided with the cabal. Some said he was eyeing the coveted Negro vote, but Vinnie felt sure he saw things through the lens of her beloved Mr. Lincoln.

Johnson backed the reconstruction of the South as Lincoln would have desired. This led to a battle between the President and Congress. Many senators who had been elected on the call for vengeance against the defeated South wanted a mean and revengeful type of reconstruction. One of these was a Senator named Thaddeus Stevens, a mean-minded man who headed the cabal and later became the prime mover in the impeachment proceedings against Johnson. It was he who was behind the vilification of Vinnie Ream, resulting in the closure of her studio.

Vinnie had been sponsored by a Senator Ross when she came to Washington. This elderly man had fallen in love with her and was essential to the ends of the political intrigue.

Thaddeus Stevens decided to use Vinnie. Either she must persuade him to join the cabal or she would lose her commission for the statue. He minced no words in this blackmail.

Here was a test of her mettle! In her dilemma, she went to a local spiritualist. She received assurances that the murdered President was "working" in her behalf in the beyond, and that right would prevail.

It was known that the vote of Senator Ross would swing the impeachment decision either way. It was either President Johnson or Vinnie's future, but she knew what Lincoln wanted her to do. She used all her influence with the aging Senator Ross, who was not hard for her to handle, to vote against conviction of Johnson. The result of the count was, as history records, nineteen against and eighteen for. Johnson was saved. Of course, Vinnie's commission was cancelled.

When President Johnson was reinstated he ordered the statue of Lincoln to be completed. Her work in Washington finished, Vinnie eventually went to live abroad with her husband, where she executed many more excellent works. She returned home to die at age 67 in her birthplace, Madison, Wisconsin.

LINCOLN'S DREAM

Abraham Lincoln's belief in superstitions is well-known, but not enough attention has been paid by his biographers to the significance which the number seven played throughout his career. He considered it his lucky number. His Christian name and surname each have seven letters; he became a member of the House of Representatives on December 17, 1847; he was elected by the people seven times (four times to the Illinois Legislature, once to the House of Representatives and twice to the Presidency); he was shot on April 14 (7 times 2), and his body left Washington on April 21 (7 times 3).

Mrs. Lincoln recalled some very strange incidents of occult origin after her husband's murder. Once in Springfield, for example, just before the election of 1860, she saw a double reflection of Lincoln in a mirror, one quite lifelike and the other ghostly. And this peculiar dual image appeared again just before they left the White House for Ford's Theater on the fatal night of his assassination.

As if clairvoyant, Lincoln brooded over his end. His law partner, Herndon, records that Lincoln said to him several times over a period of twenty years: "I am sure that I shall meet with a terrible end." In Philadelphia in 1861, at Liberty Hall, touching the principle of the Declaration of Independence, he said: "If this country cannot be saved without giving up that principle . . . I would rather be assassinated on this very spot than surrender it." Four years later it was there that his body lay in state.

Perhaps the strangest premonition that the Great Liberator ever had was a dream which he himself recorded on a piece of paper about ten days before he died and which was found on his desk afterwards. The prose bears the mark of his unmistakable lapidary style.

"About one week ago," he writes, "I retired very late. I could not have been in bed very long when I fell into a slumber, for I was very weary. I soon began to dream. There seemed to be a deathlike stillness about me. Then I heard subdued sobs, as if a number of people were weeping. I thought I left my bed and wandered downstairs. There the silence was broken by the same pitiful sobbing, but the mourners were invisible. I was puzzled and alarmed. What could be the meaning of all this? Determined to find the cause of a state of things so mysterious and shocking, I kept on until I arrived at the East Room and entered.

"There I met with a sickening surprise. Before me was a catafalque on which rested a corpse wrapped in funeral vestments. Around it were stationed soldiers who were acting as guards; and there was a throng of people, some gazing mournfully at the corpse, whose face was covered; others were weeping pitifully. 'Who is dead in the White House?' I demanded of the soldiers. 'The President,' was the answer. 'He was killed by an assassin's bullet.' Then came a loud burst of grief from the crowd which awoke me from my dream. I slept no more that night; and although it was only a dream, I have been strangely disturbed by it ever since."

ESOTERIC THIRTEEN

We are all familiar with the unpopularity of the number thirteen. We know it is often omitted from office buildings and from housing complexes, often ridiculously substituting 11a or 12a in its place. The superstition dies hard because it was probably founded after the Last Supper where Judas was the thirteenth person present. But many numerologists are becoming aware, if gradually, that it is more lucky than otherwise, despite many anecdotes to the contrary. It has, moreover, great significance for the destiny of the U.S.A.

In my book *It's Better in America* I devoted a chapter to John Hanson (1715-1783), the first man to hold the title of President of the United States (this was before the advent of George Washington as such—when the Thirteen Colonies first became known as the United States and Mr. Hanson was President of the so-called Continental Congress). He was also a First Degree Scottish Mason. He supervised the design of the Great Seal of the United States and because of him we have the number thirteen utilized throughout this fine piece of national heraldry.

Others who worked on the project were also Masons and were aware that the United States had been born astrological-ly with the number thirteen as its mass-chord vibration. Incidentally, the number made its debut with the Thirteen Colonies before the Great Seal existed. Thirteen generals of the Revolutionary War were Freemasons, with George Washington Master of their Lodge.

This explains the symbols of Masonry which are used so prominently in the Seal. Look at any one-dollar bill and you will see on one side of it the top of the pyramid, the all-seeing eye of God surrounded by a haze of light. The motto *Annuit Coeptus* has thirteen letters. This capstone is detached from the main edifice and looks down on its thirteen structures, with the date 1776 in Roman letters. To the right side of this somber pyramid is the image of the spread eagle with wings of thirteen feathers each. The bird holds an olive branch of thirteen leaves in one of its claws, and in the other thirteen arrows. Above the head are thirteen stars, over a scroll inscribed with the Latin of Virgil, *E Pluribus Unum*, containing thirteen letters.

The numeral thirteen was also carried out with the design of the Mace, used still in the House of Representatives, with thirteen ebony rods bound together by bands of silver. On the national shield, thirteen bars are joined to a larger one across the breast of that particular eagle.

Many important birthdays in the U.S. have fallen on the thirteenth and this number has influenced the country's history. Obviously this number has sympathetic interchanges, so do all the digits when paired. In the case of thirteen they involve the numbers one and four. Here are a few examples, but anyone, better schooled in American history than myself, can find many more:

Washington's Birthday: February 22 = 4
Declaration of Independence: July 4
Birthday of George III: July 4
(who brought on the Revolution)
Continental Congress founded: May 10 = 1
First order of Civil War: April 13
Fort Sumter surrendered: April 13
Battle of Donaldson: February 13
Battle of Fredericksburg: December 13
Dewey entered Manila Bay: May 1
Capture of Manila: August 13
President Wilson born: May 28 = 1
(Mr. Wilson shortened his name to 13 letters)
Gen. John J. Pershing born: June 13
(His name adds up to thirteen letters)
President Wilson arrived in France: December 13
First convoy of ships to help Allies sailed: June 13
Decisive Battle of St. Mihiel won by U.S.: September 13

Apollo 13 came down safely the 13th of the month

In an ancient book on numbers it is stated "He who understands the sum of ten plus three will find it useful for dominion. It represents a new age and a new order which makes things favorable for experimentation and development." Does this not chime with the psychological climate of the U.S.A.?

Among famous people who found thirteen important in their lives were two composers, Richard Wagner and Arnold Schoenberg. Wagner was especially happy with it, Schoenberg not. Born in 1813, Wagner was given thirteen letters in his name. He composed a total of thirteen operas, the best of which (in the opinion of many), *Tannhauser*, was given its premiere at the Paris Opera House on March 13, 1845. He began *Parsifal* (his last work) on Good Friday, 1857, which fell on the 13th. This work was finished on January 13th. 1882 after many distractions, mainly ill health. The first performance of his *Ring* cycle was given at Beyreuth on August 13th. 1876. He left Beyreuth for Venice on January 13th. 1883 and died on February 13th. of a heart embolism, which contains thirteen letters. He stated that he had always planned his life to make important decisions on the 13th. day wherever possible.

Arnold Schoenberg spent his life fearful of the number. He was born on September 13th. 1874. Instead of accepting this as a matter of fatalistic significance and letting the esoterics of the number work themselves out, as Wagner had done, Schoenberg fought against it and allowed the mysterious coincidences to make him miserable.

He believed that the number 13 was inimical to his luck and, in thinking so, he may have courted misfortune with it. At first he was mainly afraid of multiples of the number. Every birthday which gave this result would make him heave a sigh of relief when the next year came. "I have survived!" he would repeat each time. To try to break his belief in the superstition, his wife urged him to compose a work in 1913 called *The Lucky Hand,* a piece for the theater—but he had no luck with its production.

Over a period of years he worked on what some critics feel is his best work, *Gurre-Lieder*. Fate decreed that it would be performed for the first time on September 13, 1913 and conducted by the celebrated Franz Schreker (thirteen letters), in Vienna. It was received badly by hostile criticisms. Now it is regarded as a masterpiece! A little later he began his Twelve Tone method of musical composition, bringing his name to world attention. This, oddly enough, involves a combination of tones known as Chord the Thirteenth.

Schoenberg and his family arrived in the U.S.A. as refugees from the Nazis on the last day of the month, having sailed on the 13th. in 1933. A festival of his works was held at the Denver (Colorado) Art Museum, on October 13th. 1937 and received with mixed criticisms. When he reached the age of 65, he felt sure he would die because it made a multiple of thirteen. A noted numerologist finally advised him that the age marked for his death would probably add up to this number. Schoenberg died on July 13th. 1951, aged 76— which two digits add up to thirteen.

In spite of his own feelings, the number did not interfere with his being considered today one of the greatest, if most controversial, modern composers. He is a marvelous example of what opposition to tradition can accomplish. He proved again that the dissonance of today is the consonance of tomorrow! He simply could not see the consonance in the number 13!

The first Health Insurance Act in the world, which was to bring succour to many millions of people, was started in 1913. Prime Minister Lloyd George, a believer in the pseudo-science of Numerology, insisted that the card, upon which payment stamps were to be affixed, have thirteen spaces. He arranged for the stamps to cost 9 pence and 4 pence each, which adds up to thirteen! Under the rules, the benefits were to cease if the contributor became thirteen weeks in arrears. This Health Insurance was a resounding success and was widely copied in several countries.

In spite of all the proof in favor of thirteen as a lucky number, sentiments against it go to ridiculous lengths. No one likes to sit down to a meal with that number present. In France every leading hostess has what is known as a list of *Quartoziennes,* which are potential guests who can be called upon to be the fourteenth in emergency!

PSYCHOKINESIS AND THE EVIL EYE

In her fascinating book, *The Hidden Springs,* Renée Haynes, a Council member of the Society for Psychical Research, has included a chapter on the Evil Eye, the oldest superstition in the world. Rightly, she links this power with psycho-kinesis, the influence of mind upon matter with or without physical instrumentation. She states that there are two distinct types of this terrible affliction, the first being known as *malacchio* and thought to be a voluntary and deliberate form of cursing. The better known (and the most prevalent) is called the *jettatura,* still feared in Greece and Italy. In the latter country a group of psychiatrists are studying the possibility it may be related to certain cases of persons who are accident prone. These victims of this sinister misfortune are not aware they possess the power of bringing untoward events to themselves as well as to others.

Every insurance statistician is familiar with the person who has more than the normal number of accidents or tragedies. It is no respecter of social class and there is a Grecian princess still living said to be a victim. Her husband died of a monkey bite while playing with her pet. Their daughter married a European king, who lost his throne soon afterwards. Rumor has it that wherever the princess is something unfortunate occurs. The electricity fails during a stay with friends; or a main waterpipe floods the hotel where she is putting up. Without being aware of it, the lady brings trouble to all and sundry so, naturally, her friends feel she might be afflicted with the *jettatura.* They will warn you not to look her too closely in the eyes!

I have written in my book *Who's There?* about the Irish sorceress who cursed the Kennedy family in 1848 and has caused such tragedies to it, even down to the present hour. A similar case happened in the Breadalbane family, owners of a Scottish earldom since 1677. The title was bestowed on Sir John Campbell by King Charles the Second for bringing law and order for the Crown in Caithness. The new Earl of Breadalbane finally issued an order to burn all witches in his domain.

One of these was an ugly old woman "with dark glaring eyes so sinister as to strike fear in all beholders," who inhabited Loch Tay. As she died under the crackling flames, she screamed a curse resounding in the Breadalbane family for many generations. "I suffer now," she mouthed in her agony, "but the Breadalbanes will suffer always. Long may their name last, and wide may their lands be, but never shall their heirs inherit from father to son!"

The first Earl of Breadalbane may have mocked the poor sufferer. If he did, time, that inexorable avenger, was not slow in proving him wrong. His son went insane and died before he did. By special arrangement with King Charles, the letters patent were altered to include a clause in favor of the heirs male-general, that is to say the title could devolve onto any kinsmen. In this way Lord Breadalbane was more likely to outwit the curse and his title would continue.

Accidents, diseases, and wars have carried off, in a most relentless way, the potential heirs in this tragic family. The third earl died of a mysterious illness which could not be diagnosed and he left no issue. The honor was inherited by his cousin, Sir Robert Campbell. The only son of this gentleman died in infancy of a fall from his cot. The fifth earl was found dead in a lonely copse where he had been shooting rabbits. He, too, left no issue so that a Campbell cousin succeeded him. This incumbent died without kin and it looked as if the witch's curse had finally run its course and made the family extinct.

Some years later, in 1872, a John Alexander Campbell filed a claim with the House of Lords in an effort to take the title out of abeyance. He was able to prove that he was a very distant collateral of the family. On the strength of this he was granted permission to inherit the title and estates in Caithness, at that time 365,000 acres. Evidently he planned to raise a large family and in preparation for it enlarged the castle by the addition of a new wing. Yet he died childless. A kinsman inherited from him, becoming the seventh earl, but he also died without male issue.

The same fate was in store for the eighth earl, Charles William Campbell, who died in 1923. He made every effort to beat the curse by insisting that his nephew and heir, Ian Herbert Campbell, should marry early and thus sire himself an heir since his own wife had been unable to bless him with a son. It was therefore with considerable alacrity that the reigning earl learned that his great-nephew had been born on 28th. April 1919. Doubtless the old earl died happy in the thought that the witch might at long last be ditched.

The ninth earl died in 1959, doubtless with a sigh of relief that his son, Lord Glenorchy, would be the tenth earl—the first to inherit from father to son since the old hag on Loch Tay had caused the impasse. The present Earl of Breadalbane married his wife, Coralie Archer, in 1949. Up to the time of writing she has been unable to produce an heir and since Lord Breadalbane states they are madly in love with each other, it does not seem likely he will divorce and remarry. The witch may have the last cackling laugh and the title may yet become extinct. There is no kinsman left to inherit it.

That happened to the ancient Scottish family of the Mackintosh of Moy. In olden times a Mackintosh killed the father and brother of the Chatham heiress, whom he brought to the bloody scene. She was said to possess occult powers of "eyeing" her enemies. Moreover, she must have been a poetess for she put her curse into rhyme:

Never the son of a Chief of Moy
May live to protect his father's age,
Or close in peace his dying eye,
Or gather his gloomy heritage.

The ill-wishing worked throughout the centuries. With monotonous regularity no Chief of Moy has been succeeded by his own son. One by one they have lived to bury their

131

male heirs. Finally, the family of Mackintosh ran out of kinsmen and became extinct.

The evil eye once inhabited a portrait! In the year 1615 Pieter Bruegel (1564-1637) exhibited at a Brussels gallery a work of a female freak of nature entitled "Possessor of Devils." It was so alive with supernatural sorcery that some viewers complained it had an evil effect on them; and the owners quickly sold it to a local antiquarian. This man soon suffered bad luck. Browsers would leave his shop in fright, insisting the fire of the terrifying eyes upset them. Bruegel was threatened with condemnation by the Inquisition and ordered to burn the canvas, which he did. Here was his story:

He had seen the model selling flowers on a street corner. Her vicious and macabre appearance suggested a character for a portrait. He asked her to pose and she agreed, although she was obviously very ill. As he put in the first shadows of her features the creative surge seemed to pour from the wicked brain of the sitter. Without effort his brush picked up the willful look of cursing in the eyes. He finished the work in half an hour.

Suddenly the creature raised herself from her chair and shrieked: "Look at your painting, Artist!" And obediently Bruegel moved away, leaping back further in horror. From the hideous face he had painted he now saw a pair of living eyes popping out of their sockets in all their madness. "You see," continued the hag, "my life has gone into your canvas. My body is about to die, but this painting and I will never part!"

And then she fell dead, leaving Pieter Bruegel to take her corpse to the mortuary. From this time on, he gave up his profane portrait studies and took to religious subjects which are represented in museums all over the world.

SECTION FIVE

A MYSTICAL EXPERIENCE

From what psychologists now know, the brain never rests and some form of psychic activity goes on continually, if only of the most subdued kind. During my period of work with Maurice Maeterlinck, he said to me one morning "I believe our intuitions from the inner consciousness are really the veiled guides sent to steer our course through life, though many find themselves handicapped to speak of them. Here is a story which delves down into their most unfathomable depths, throwing a flood of light on the darkest recesses of the human soul."

I made notes from the outline he gave me and we planned to develop it for publication, but other work supervened. I set it down for the first time now, filling in certain lacunae to make it more storyable. I should say at the start that Maeterlinck spoke only of "Emile," not giving me the surname of his friend involved, but I suspected it was Emile Verhaeren (1855-1904), who had been one of his greatest friends. Another reason for my thinking so was because some of the great Belgian writer's work was obsessed with a stretch of sandy sea-coast which lies between the North Sea and the estuary of the Scheldt river, near Antwerp. This was the background for part of the psychical experience and, in passing, I might add that Verhaeren pictures incisively the characters of this district's narrow minded citizens, with all their smugness, avarice, and hypocricy.

Maeterlinck described Emile as being shy and retiring, an

enemy of self-advertisement, which fits the reputation of Verhaeren. He was killed tragically in a train accident after finishing, oddly enough, a poem about trains seen at night, ending with the lovely line "The glittering golden galleons of the tracks."

So here is the story, told to Maeterlinck by Emile about fifty years earlier and retold to me in 1943. Emile began:

"I have never told you of my early life because much of it is very sad. I would like to do so now because I know you believe that what happens to us in life is arbitrarily set afoot by thoughts we shelter within the deep recesses of our being. Whence comes the shadow of certain events which makes our lives so hard to bear?

"Have you noticed how the soul sometimes converts its psychical phenomena into an ill-defined pattern for the future? I am convinced that he who learns to interpret the omens of dreams can retrace in himself important periods of passion and crisis, as well as aberrations of the mind. Anyway, I have proved to myself that my subconscious mind was able to penetrate my ignorance of the past.

"As you know, the public believes I am a Belgian and, for the first twenty-one years of my life so did I! You see, my father and mother died when I was not yet two years old. I was then put in the charge of an elderly uncle who lived in old Salem, Massachusetts. How I arrived there, I never knew, but I must have been taken there by a guardian. My uncle was kind enough, as best I can recall him. He is only a vague picture in my memory. Great veins traversed his forehead which was vast and domed like the front of a chapel. Beneath his large nostrils was a moustache, blackened by snuff. The poor man was so enormously fat that he would seemingly overflow the huge stuffed chairs in which he sat all day long. I cannot remember one word he uttered. My main memory of him is of his immense weight, which killed him in the end.

"I know I must have stayed with Uncle Toland for over a year—anyway until his death. At that time I was sent to the local Roman Catholic orphanage. There, surrounded by forbidding walls, I remained for many drab years with other

134

homeless or abandoned children. It was to be my home until I came of legal age. I can still remember toddling along those austere passages and sleeping in the draughty dormitories with their dark, vaulted alcoves. Life became a succession of tedious religious activities. Patiently we all joined in the acts of atonement to the Sacrament. The special services we were compelled to attend were as countless as the stars we watched in the heavens at night.

"It was a comfortless existence, with no motherly face or hands to console us and no ties to bind us to the past which, for me, was non-existent. My only consolation was in the fact that there were others in similar circumstances. One exception was Walter, a friend I made in later years, a boy with joyous smiles and pale eyes. I believe we took to each other not only because we were both the same age but also because of our interest in good books.

"We were both emaciated seventeen-year-olds but in his case the cloistral life, with its unrelieved boredom, had not registered on his features as much as it had on mine. This was perhaps because of periodic visits to a close relative who lived at Cohasset, a nearby seaside resort.

"I have always suffered from chronic bronchial attacks which still make many nights hideous. The orphanage doctor seemed unable to help this malady, so it was especially pleasant when one day Walter invited me to pass several days with him and his Aunt. Permission was easily obtained and we went to Cohasset at Eastertide, where my life began to take on a more cheerful tone. Walter's Aunt Suzan turned out to be a warmhearted, buxom, middle-aged lady who at once showed me the maternal care previously always lacking in my young life.

"To add to this congenial atmosphere Suzan had a daughter, a pretty young woman named Annie, who was as healthy as I was unhealthy. She always dressed in blue serge which seemingly imprisoned her firm young breasts. She would enter a room spreading a fresh scent of eau-de-Cologne, lighting any place she went with the splendor of her youth and beauty. Her head was crowned with a burning mass of auburn hair. Need I tell you that I fell a willing victim to these charms?

"During the holiday Walter was absent visiting another relative and I was left alone more often with Annie. We would sit together, reading. Occasionally, she would raise the fringed curtain of her eyelashes as I waited anxiously for a glance. But all too often it would end with her eyes falling, with unfeeling coldness upon the pages of her book.

"One evening when we were nearing the end of my holiday, Annie and I were lounging aimlessly on the terrace under great lime trees, watching the tiny harbor light up like stars. We began strolling together in the lower part of the garden which was fringed by a deep and dark copse. There we sat for a few minutes on the lawns bordering a marble fountain into which Annie dropped a ring from her finger in order to make a wish. I was standing closely beside her to help her fish it out when, with a shiver of fear, I saw a strange second-self of Annie mirrored in the water. Her freckled face grew paler and paler against the gloomy dark background of the thicket. In my vivid imagination I seemed to be hearing half-uttered sighs of woe, which I attributed to the melancholy knowledge that Annie would depart next day and I would return with Walter to the orphanage. I of course had all the usual symptoms of a young man secretly and hopelessly in love. Naturally I was asking myself if I would ever meet Annie again.

"That night I was so uneasy about Annie vanishing from my life that I was unable to drop off to sleep. I casually took up a volume of poetry from the bedside table. It was the complete poetry of Thomas Hood and I was mysteriously drawn to a poem I had not read before, *Hero and Leander*. I became lost in the images of submarine visions, of Leander's descent into the sea in the loving arms of a mermaid. In graphic language the poet describes Leander sinking down further and further into the billowy deep, passing fishes with round, vacant eyes and seaweed yellow as egg yolks. In lovely rhythmic meters, Hood ends one of his verses with 'Down, and still downward through the dusky green . . .'

"And it was in this weird mood that I finally fell off to sleep. Before I lost consciousness, however, my eyes became fixed on a strangely ornamented mirror over the mantelpiece, where I seemingly saw Leander sink deeper and deeper to his fate. Then, beginning to dream, I found myself at the bottom of what was obviously a fresh water well, encompassed by rounded brick walls. In my dream's eye, I could see I was making those meaningless physical struggles to extricate myself—frustrating attempts which are a part of every nightmare and never have any counterpart in life itself. I felt that horrifying, breathless panic, so typical of nightmares, as if I were leisurely suffocating to death.

"You must be aware of the superstition which holds that a drowning man is supposed to see, as in a mirror, his entire past paraded rapidly before him. I believe many people saved from drowning have later testified that their thoughts journeyed swiftly backwards until they reached babyhood. In my case I was suddenly given, as if from nowhere, a hand-mirror to clutch. It was empty of any reflection at all. I remember being thunderstruck because I was then nearly nineteen and my life had been filled with many events, even if most of them were disagreeable.

"I can also remember seeing some very curious images around me. Mixed with the debris the images shaped up in my dreaming mind into the crude form of a woman's breast, and another looked weirdly like a baby's hand detached from its body.

"Then I realized that I had been at the bottom of the well and was now risen to the surface. Somehow I was also able to look above the well-head. Shadowed by a storm-wracked sky, I saw a woman's face hitherto unknown to me. Her expression was of great anxiety, even fright. She was making wild gestures of panic.

"I was given barely enough time to assimilate all this when, like the mirror, the face and arms disappeared. As this happened another face appeared, this time of Annie, whose features merged in montage with those of the older woman. I felt an affectionate human hand around my body, which had suddenly become ridiculously small, the size of a baby. Without difficulty I was removed from the water and I forcibly felt the keen relief of being able to breathe oxygen once more. Above was a waterlogged sky and the air was fretting with dampness. But I was happily distracted by the loving hands which were hugging me as they dried off my shivering little body. I heard words of affection in a language I was too young to understand.

"Clothing me with a large blanket, this lady took me into her arms, passing through the garden into the street outside. But instead of it being the street fronting Aunt Suzan's home or even the street outside the orphanage, it was quite unknown to me. In the dismal rainfall I noticed white walls of what looked like a convent with forbidding black blinds drawn. Two enormous zinc gutters, one on either side of the slated roof, were gushing water. On the other side of the street was a sea of terraced roofs. Some had cupolas shaped like ovens. Above all was the stormracked sky, somber and terrifying.

"I was held tightly by my benefactor as we passed canals, quaysides, and a pair of drawbridges, holding up their arms, as if in fright. The familiar Massachusetts scenery was nowhere. On the horizon, there appeared two black windmills, their gigantic sails motionless.

"I turned my tiny head to take a second look at these strange landmarks. Wriggling within the arms enclosing me, I awoke from this dream with a start. I had struck my skull against the headboards of my bed. I gave a sigh of relief that this was only a dream!

"At once I tried to analyze my dream, if only to give it a form of semi-reality. One thing was clear. This was no excursion into limbo, nor a welcome deliverance from my waking prison. In other of my dreams I have become the plaything of unknown variations and caprices, but not in this one. Another mystery was that my dream could not have been retrospective because the hand-mirror reflected nothing. I had to classify it as a jumble of events, a fragile puzzle that could have emanated from my mystical colloquy with Annie by the fountain, when she threw her ring into the water. So I went back to sleep.

"At breakfast, later on, I found regretfully that my beloved Annie had already gone to join Walter in New Haven. I felt this rather keenly since she had not bothered to wake me, as she had promised, to say farewell. Of course, we were not then aware that we would never meet again. I lost no time in writing her a letter in which I told her that I loved her. Then I said, 'By the by, Annie, I dreamt of you last night, but it was a strange, strange you. It was as if you were a mixture of two different personalities, one of whom was much older, yet the other unmistakably had your lovely face. I was drowning and found myself at the bottom of a well. When I surfaced, I saw your face at its head. Your face then changed magically to that of the older woman, waving her arms frantically, but they were not a part of her body! Oddest thing of all, this older woman began uttering several times a sentence which sounded like "the kind is in the pit!"

"Next, I was pulled to safety but it was not the me as I am today. I was a small child and a sorry spectacle. I assure you the voice which cried out was your voice, Annie. If you had waked me to say goodbye, as you promised to do, maybe I would never have been visited by this disturbing experience. I must gently chide you!'

"This letter never reached Annie due to a mistake in the New Haven address. I still have the envelope which was franked October 25th, 1880. It was returned to me and I shall always keep it as a memento.

"In due course I returned to the orphanage. Time there passed slowly but finally I attained my majority and came into my inheritance. This event was ushered in by the receipt of a mass of papers from a firm of lawyers at Utrecht. Due to the strict practice at the orphanage never to reveal to the inmates their true family background, I was still in ignorance of mine.

"Therefore, I was flabbergasted to discover that my father and mother had been Dutch. It transpired that my father went to the Colonies and died there when I was less than

139

eighteen months old. My poor mother died shortly afterwards in Utrecht. She had remained there because of my imminent birth and her delicate health. It also came out in these papers that she and I were scheduled to leave for Java in the near future when her death intervened and I was sent to the distant relative in Massachusetts.

"I was further informed I was heir to the family dwelling in Utrecht and a valuable piece of property in Java which could realize a considerable sum when sold. Then my eyes fell upon information that would help later to solve the mystery of my dream at Cohasset. It was a signed receipt by the now celebrated Belgian artist, Francis Navez (1787-1869) for the sum of twelve florins. In his own handwriting, it stated that this was payment for a portrait he had done of my mother, dated September, 1862.

"Then, with a feeling of despair mingled with love, I came across a letter sealed and marked 'To my Lambkin.' It was long and from my mother to me, 'I am a dying woman. I had hoped to live to see you grow to manhood but my health failed. When you are old enough to read this, the cold earth will have separated us for many years. I want you to know of a near fatal accident which happened to you when a baby. The doctor told me it may cause you to suffer chronic bronchial trouble later one. You see, some time ago I took you to call on a neighbor, Madame van Brammen, who lives at 33 Oude Street. You were just learning to toddle. We left you in charge of Sarthe, Madame van Brammen's younger daughter. She took you into the garden and momentarily left you on the lawn so she could fetch you a glass of milk. But when she returned you had vanished!

"Instinctively Sarthe ran to the well-head and looked down. There you were, poor darling, miraculously floating. Instead of trying to pull you out, she came screaming to the window where Madame van Brammen and I were gossiping inside. She was shouting, 'The kind is in the put!' Since this is Dutch you may not understand it. Translated it means, 'The child is in the well!' Of course Madame van Brammen and I went to your rescue and pulled out your struggling little body. We did our best to shake the water out of your lungs and I took you quickly to the nearest doctor. So guard your lungs, dear boy.

"How I wish I could keep you always near to my heart, but a case of rapid cancer is killing me. You will be sent to Uncle Toland, a kindly, if eccentric man, in faraway America, where I have never been, nor never shall go.'

"A lump formed in my throat. I was struck by the fact that there is no message more pathetic than that which reaches the recipient after the hand which penned it had been stilled. My dear mother spoke to me in a ghostly voice in words which rang with sighing melancholy.

"This letter certainly explained my continual bouts of bronchitis as well as the haunting dream, which must now take on deeper significance. I need hardly tell you that I lost no time in bidding the orphange authorities farewell, after which I took the ship for Holland to attend my affairs.

"There I sought out my mother's home, which was located on the Stingel, near the Parvendel on the outskirts of Utrecht. It was tenanted by two maiden ladies to whom I gave notice to leave so that I could sell it. They were of course annoyed at me. I was very curious to see the house where Madame van Brammen lived, which address my mother had given me. As I was wending my way to it, there were the two windmills of my dream, one in motion and the other sailless. Both now were sending messages to me from the past!

"As I suspected, Madame van Brammen had died some years before. The present owner spoke tolerable English and was uniformly polite. He agreed to let me see the garden, where instinctively I knew the location of the well. Gravely, the new owner told me that since water was made available from the city mains, it was no longer in use. Pointing to a wrought-iron grill over its head, he casually remarked that this was installed many years ago when a child was very nearly drowned.

"The grill did not completely hide the inside, now mossy with age. I stood transfixed by the scene where my brief life

141

might so easily have ended, asking myself if it would have been better had I not risen to the surface? To the world I am now famous and successful, but I alone know the price. I was quickly interrupted by the owner asking me if I would like to see the inside of the house.

"By request I took the tour alone, guided by what seemed like my mother's spirit. I wandered from room to room, finally entering the high-ceilinged ante-chamber which Madame van Brammen probably used for withdrawing into. At the far end was an alcove with bow windows looking northward upon a sprightly row of trees. The alcove was raised, like a dais, with a charming curved seat built around the windows. Above the seat was a portrait in a place of honor. At first glance it reminded me of Annie, but the face was much older and a trifle paler. Above all, I knew I had seen the face somewhere before. In a flash, it was all made clear to me. Here was the woman's face I had seen in my dream at the mouth of the well!

"Carefully I examined the portrait and was able to decipher the signature, now yellowed and faded. It read 'Francois Navez, 1859.' Here was my dear mother although I had never seen a likeness of her. Why the picture had not been willed to me, I cannot say. I can only suppose that Madame van Brammen bought it from the estate to keep as a memento. What struck me most was the amazing resemblance between my mother and the memory of Annie's features. There was the same look of soul, the similar ethereal countenance.

"This discovery prompted me to check on other aspects of my dream. (Did I forget to tell you that its haunting me has always been the strongest during bad weather?) I went to the offices of the Utrecht *Courant*. In the files for the issue of September 18th, 1862 (the day after my accident at the well), there was this item:

Yesterday at about six o'clock the sloop *Faithful Helen* broke her moorings due to a sudden squall. The violence of the winds blew it aground where she struck an anchored tjalk from Vlissengen in the Willen's Kade. Captain Milford de

Goole reported the damage was not inconsiderable.

"The storm clinched all the details I needed for my dream to prove all its prophesy and predestination. In a way, it transformed the pattern of my life, proving to me that the subconscious mind, so subtle and powerful, is able to penetrate the veil of the unknown past. Indeed, I now ask myself, without having died, am I already a ghost?"

PHANTASMS ACROSS THE SEA

The word phantasm was invented for the psychical vocabulary to refer to the etheric counterpart of the physical body in its power to move in space, with comparative freedom, and to appear very briefly in varying degrees of density to others, usually during a state of crisis. It is also known as projection of the astral double or bilocation. One of the early accomplishments of the Psychical Research Society in London was the compilation of many hundreds of such cases, which were told in all the frightening details. *Phantasms of the Living* was published by three of the Society's founders, Frederic W.H. Myers, Frank Podmore, and Edmund Gurney, in 1885.

Here are two impressive examples of this type of phenomenon which were given to me by personal friends, both of which involve life-size projections at the time of death across the trackless and unending swells of the Atlantic. The first was told to me by Mrs. Ben Webster (Dame May Whitty), who died in Hollywood in 1948. She was titled by her king for her work on the London stage, then came to New York and Hollywood, where she was in demand as a character actress.

Ben Webster, her husband and also an actor of note, was the grandson of a famous actor-producer with the same name who lived from 1797-1882 and was known for his great versatility. His friend and collaborator on several London theatrical projects was Tyrone Power born the same year. He was a great-grandfather of Tyrone Power, the Hollywood matinee idol, who died in 1958.

The time finally came when Tyrone Power's great-grandfather received offers to come to the U.S.A., where he was an immediate success—portraying Irish buffoons, such as Larry Hollogan O'Halloran. In the early part of 1841 he decided to return to his family in England for a well-earned rest. A mutual friend of his and the Ben Websters saw him off aboard the S.S. *President* which sailed from New York Harbor on March 13th, 1841. Casually, Mr. Power mentioned to his friend that he had just invested the money he had made on the New York stage in some real estate in mid-Manhattan. He said that a local lawyer was handling the matter for him, but he gave no name.

Off the coast of Nantucket Island, the S.S. *President* ran into a tempestuous gale and foundered in the early hours of the next morning, with all souls lost. At about the equivalent time, Mr. Webster was sleeping soundly in his London home, when loud thumps came to his front door. He went to the window and saw, standing in the pelting rain, the drenched figure of Tyrone Power, who had often been at that portal before. Naturally, Mr. Webster was startled because he thought Mr. Power was still in America. A voice came up which was unmistakably that of his old friend. "Let me in, Ben. I'm drowning! I've something important to tell you."

Hastily, Ben Webster went downstairs and unbolted the door, but no sign of Tyrone Power, only downpouring rain. In those days there was no wireless for messages across the sea and it took a few weeks for the sad news to arrive. London theatrical circles were stunned, and then a letter came to Mrs. Power—from the friend who last saw her husband alive. He spoke of the real estate her husband had bought. At once she put through an inquiry and a search was made in every way. Neither the lawyer, who was said to be handling the matter, nor the property itself, could be traced.

The apparition appeared at about the same time as the severance of Mr. Power's spirit from his physical body was taking place. Dame May Whitty, a superstitious person, wondered if her husband's grandfather was trying to communicate the missing information. She felt that possibly death by drowning weakens the power to project the astral double, otherwise Mr. Power might have been able to stay longer and perhaps solve the mystery of the American investment.

The name of Pola Negri conjures up nostalgia. She was a *femme fatale* in Hollywood films just before they were taught to talk. Pola and I have been friends since 1930 and, I am happy to say, we still keep closely in touch since her voluntary retirement to San Antonio, Texas. To her admirers, she was lovable, generous, and harmonious. Her enemies thought her imperious, demanding, and arrogant. Some directors called her a "nightmare" because of her tantrums, but I have always found her courteous and kind. She now allows me to print this story, which tells of another phantasm across the sea, in which she was the percipient.

Before she came to the U.S.A., one of her ardent admirers was a handsome Polish engineer to whom she was much attached. A little later his work took him to another country where he expected to remain. This pleased Pola's mother, who did not approve of him. A painful parting took place between the lovers as he took the train to Warsaw.

"I'll be back, and if you are not here I'll come wherever you are! I am going to make a success of myself and your mother will have no more to say. And even if I die, Pola, I'll come to you. Or if you die first, will you come to me?"

They had laughed at this last promise. Then Pola tried to speak affirmatively, but her voice failed and her eyes suddenly filled with tears. The whistle blew and the train chugged out of the station.

For some time they exchanged letters and their thoughts and longings came as mental communications—that wavelength which love builds between two hearts. Ultimately Pola was contracted to go to Hollywood and magic-lantern changes took place in her life. She became one of the leading Hollywood stars in some excellent films and the memory of the passionate love affair with the Polish engineer was forgotten. He was able, however, to keep in touch with news of her from the papers. He read that she had fallen madly in love with a man whose name was on the lips of every woman, the dashing Rudolph Valentino, and he with her. The rejected lover did write to say he wished her well and that his love still burned with an unextinguished flame.

One evening, many years later, the famous actress was reading the evening newspaper in the drawing room of her spacious Beverly Hills home, when she felt a strange impulse to look behind her. She turned her head and saw that the door had been silently opened and near a large antique couch stood a figure which she quickly recognized as her former admirer.

With a smile of delight, she rose to greet him, exclaiming: "How could you come without letting me know? I had no idea you were in America!"

But the man moved his hand sadly in a way that forbade approach. Miss Negri remained rooted to where she stood as he advanced a small step towards her. He did not reply, only gestured in such a way as to register despair.

At once Miss Negri remembered the compact and she realized that he must be fulfilling it, as the figure made to leave, waving a pathetic farewell. She wrote immediately to Poland where word came back that her friend had died in the Polish city of Poznan, where he had been injured in an engineering construction. His death was very close to the time when he made his phantasm appearance in Beverly Hills, California.

THE IRISH SAINT OF LUNACY

Sometime in the seventh century there was born at Lavey, County Cavan, a daughter to the Irish King Damaan. She was named Dymphna and eventually became as much renowned for her piety as for her beauty. The young woman had been touched by the teachings of Saint Patrick, although Christianity was not yet firmly established in Ireland and her father was still a pagan. When his wife died he decided to exercise his Royal prerogative, under the Brehon laws, to marry his daughter. She flatly refused, insisting that she wanted only the life of sanctity.

Angered by the refusal and instigated by the devil, the King made threats against her life. The princess took refuge at a nearby monastery where she was given the protection of a monk named Geburnus. Escape was the only hope for her, and together they set sail from Ireland in a curragh—arriving at what was then the Netherlands, after a hazadous journey. They were given haven at a village in Flanders named Gheel, where her father tracked them down and martyred both of them with his sword.

News of the horrible crime spread far and wide and sympathizers came to pay homage to the devout couple. Among these were two people alienated in mind, who were miraculously cured after coming to the grave of Dymphna. Soon it was reputed that her bones were radiating to cure the insane and lunatics from nearby towns were brought to a shrine that was erected for her remains. Many cures were effected and the shrine became so crowded with her worshipers a Church was built in her memory, which stands today and contains a mysterious-looking statue of her likeness. Her beatification in Rome followed and Dymphna became the Patroness of Lunacy.

So many lunatics were brought to be cured that the local clergy prevailed on the residents to board them in their homes. Gheel became known as the one and only shrine for the mentally afflicted and is today still devoted to the care of the insane. It is a town of ten thousand people run for lunatics by lunatics! In the heart of the placid Campine countryside several thousand of them live on the most cordial terms with the local inhabitants in their homes. Every resident takes a quota of mentally afflicted patients, some of them work in the fields or in the rustic workshops, and are paid small salaries. They are all treated as members of the family until they might suffer a crisis, when they are sent briefly to a central institution run by the Belgian Government.

In the enjoyment of comparative liberty and what is now called the open door system, most of the patients graduate to the outside world in due course. Such cures might take much longer in the average asylum, where regimentation would lack the sympathy of the family life offered at Gheel. The colony is supervized by an eminent psychiatrist appointed by the State and the town is subsidized by it.

Not far from Brussels, Gheel is open to the public. When I visited it some years ago, I found little to distinguish it from any other large Flemish village. The principle square is tree-lined, surrounded by undistinguished architecture. Many of the homes are of plain brick, others are stuccoed in white. There is the usual terraced garden-park, where patients meet and gossip. The farmhouses are neat, constructed of wattle or wicker ware, laid over with mud, covered with whitewashed plaster. Outlying are a few hamlets, belonging to the commune, on the edges of a sandy waste.

St. Dymphna, now listed in the Book of Saints, had no idea that her father's insane and incestuous passions would be responsible for this haven, through her consecrated to the relief of mental disease. It is another example that out of evil comes good, but there is more than that to her inspiring story. Her astonishing achievement was due to a spiritual call and vision. She was merely the medium.

MODERN EXORCISM

Possession by demons was once the theory of all insanity and the only known cure was exorcism. This was a horrible ordeal for the possessed, who was bound hand and foot in a chair, then given "holy potions" which produced moaning and fainting—until it was felt the devil was losing his control of the person. By the side of the tortured victim the exorcist would stand, reciting from religious rituals. If all this failed, burning brimstone would be held to the patient's nostrils. No wonder the exorcist's chair was dreaded worse than insanity itself!

For many years in New York, Dr. Titus Bull, a physician with a distinguished career, treated cases of insanity with the aid of trance mediums, whom he used for pleading with the possessing demons to withdraw into their ethereal world. Dr. Bull died in 1947 and, as far as I know, no one has continued his methods, which involve no more discomfort than the therapeutic devices of psychoanalysis.

Dr. Bull's theory was that certain cases of insanity were caused by the spirit being infested with non-physical entities, in the same way that the body can become the host to innumerable germs. Only cases where normal therapy had failed were taken by Dr. Bull for spirit intercession. Those of arrested mental growth or organic brain disease do not come within the orbit of exorcism.

A possessing demon was defined by Dr. Bull as the spirit or ghost of an undeveloped individual, that is a person who had not controlled the passions and appetites in this life and could not leave them behind when death came. By invading a living personality this evil entity somehow gratifies them vicariously through a suggestible living person, and derives satisfaction not unlike the physical sensation known when alive.

Many of Dr. Bull's former patients are leading useful lives today. A particulary striking instance is that of a young woman who had spent years in an asylum and was diagnosed as being absolutely incurable. The onset of her condition came one day when she lapsed into a very masculine personality and began pouring out the most objectinable obscenities and bitter blasphemies. This was in contrast with her former self of virtue and charitable interest in others—but now she became susceptible to every temptation and would explain her conduct thus: "The demon is dictating to me all the time. It says: 'You could use your own mind if I let you, but I won't. You were a fool to let me get into your head, but now I'm here I am going to stay. Go on, get mad! Kill yourself if you want to. You'll never hurt me because I can go to someone else. I have control of every nerve and fiber in your body!' "

In the treatment of this sort, Dr. Bull's medium went into a trance and temporarily assumed the personality of the possessing power. Through her, the doctor would plead with the demon to leave the patient's mind. In several other cases it transpired that the invading spirit was unaware that harm was being caused, and Dr. Bull induced it to withdraw simply by impressing the fact that in harming the patient it was also harming itself.

The cases of insanity treated in this way were almost one hundred percent successful, but intercession is slow and it takes a long time—perhaps months of mediumship persuasion. Needless to say the parallel between this method and medieval exorcism is not noteworthy, but it holds out a new hope for a group of mental cases who formerly had none.

* * * * * * * * *

By reciting a ritual of the Church, we can exorcize ourselves at any time. Exclaim out loud: "Oh! Satan, enemy of mankind and rebel against heaven—who brought death to the world, who sowed discord—you, who are the root of all evil, tremble and be afraid. I command you to leave my body and go to your place of darkness."

TWO CASES OF SOMNAMBULISM

Sleep-walking is really only a dream carried into action by the percipient, but there is also an important difference from a normal night of dreaming. The somnamulist often has awareness of external objects and has been known to carry out intricate exploits without accident. Acting out a dream can either be self-induced or spontaneous. One of the most bizarre cases of alleged sleep-walking changed the law of England, inasmuch as it was accepted for evidence in a noted bastardy trial in England.

The Honorable Mrs. Christabel Russell was a client of the clairvoyant, Miss Corney, about whom I have written elsewhere. It was she who prophesied the birth of her son,

Geoffrey, who became known far and wide as "England's Dream Baby," and is the present Lord Ampthill. He was the subject of a very sensational case which went to the House of Lords and was won by his mother in by far the weirdest litigation ever to face that august body.

Before he inherited his title of Lord Ampthill, John Hugo Russell married Christabel in 1918. He fell madly in love with her youthful beauty and, to his chagrin, he found that Christabel refused him his conjugal rights. She promised to relent later on, but meanwhile insisted on a platonic relationship. In the legal proceedings that involved his later divorce, he swore that the bargain had never been broken.

The Honorable John Hugo served his country in World War One as a captain in the Royal Navy, returning to live, under the same depriving conditions, with the beautiful Christabel. Imagine his amazement when she informed him early in 1921 that she was pregnant! "This is ridiculous," he said. "You know perfectly well we have never cohabited . . ."

It was then that Christabel came up with what is a widely-quoted classic. "Oh, yes we have, my dear. You came to me during one of your sleep-walking acts. Naturally you do not remember it!"

There was no doubt that John Hugo had suffered from chronic somnabulism all his life, and one night, Christabel swore later in court, he strolled into her boudoir. Before either of them knew what was happening Geoffrey had been conceived!

John Hugo was still madly in love with Christabel, who now allowed the marriage to be normalized. But when he told his family, who disapproved of his marriage to Christabel for snobbish reasons, they were furious. He was obviously being made into a fool. They believed that Christabel had been unfaithful and that the real father was not of their blood. The ensuing divorce case rocked English society during March of 1923. After a sordid trial, a divorce verdict was entered in John Hugo's favor. Christabel consulted Miss Corney, who "saw" in her crystal ball that if she persisted she would win. She strongly urged her to go to the appellate courts. Finally, with this encouragement, Christabel took the case to the House of Lords in order to defend her son's legitimacy.

All these venerable men listened to Christabel explain the way her husband had come to her in the middle of a somnabulistic dream. Search was made for a similar case, but none was found. However, Christabel's lawyer came across a yellowing book of records 150 years old, in which a judge-made decision was that "the declaration of a father and mother cannot be admitted to cast doubt upon the issue born after marriage." The lower court's verdict was then reversed, making the battling couple still husband and wife. Another civil action followed and a decree was granted to Mr. and Mrs. Russell.

Christabel gave permission for a film to be made of the tragic-comic affair, together with Miss Corney's vital role in it. In a "crystal-balling" for Christabel's future in 1938, she issued a warning. "Beware of words ending in *itz*. The crystal ball is not clear, but any words with this ending can be serious for you. It does not matter if they are spelled *itz* or *its*."

So Mrs. Russell took heed, remembering how Miss Corney's advice had worked such wonders in the past. She stayed out of the Ritz Hotel, probably avoided fits of temper, wits, nit-wits, or perhaps concerts by Horowitz.

Then came the war, and with it two new words added to the English language ending in *itz*: Spitz and Blitz. As the fortune-teller had foreseen, these words, plus the already suspect Ritz, dealt Christabel three of the worst blows of her career. First, the man she intended to marry—the greatest love affair of her life—was killed in a Spitz aeroplane. Next, her Mayfair dress shop was destroyed in the blitz of London. Last, and perhaps cruellest, for such an ambitious woman, her legitimized son, Geoffrey, was done out of the Dukedom of Bedford, to which he was next-in-line for inheritance, by the birth of a son (Lord Tavistock) to the current duke and duchess on the 21st. February, 1940. The child was born at the Ritz Hotel in London, during an air raid, which prevented his mother going to hospital.

The scene for the next instance of an even more peculiar form of somnabulism shifts to Lake Leman in Switzerland. It involves a slumberland obsession in a psychiatric patient for Suttee, a rite by which Hindu widows used to throw themselves upon the funeral pyre of their dead husbands. It was a custom in certain parts of India until the British suppressed it; and the widow would thus commit suicide painfully, holding her husband's turban in her hands. Argument in its favor was that Suttee is a recommendation, but not a requirement, of the shastra of Hinduism.

This phenomenal somnabulism was studied between 1923 and 1924, in the nocturnal antics of a Miss Helen Smith, by Professor Flournoy, sometime head of the Department of Psychology at Geneva University, who wrote about the case in detail. Miss Smith had not much artistic education but in her sleeping activities she displayed histrionic abilities to enact scenes, totally unrelated to her waking life, with such perfection that the most accomplished actress could not have surpassed her after months of rehearsal.

It all began when she was seventeen years old and her parents consulted Dr. Flournoy about her trances during the night. They would not have worried if the girl had just walked about the house in her sleep as some sensitive young people sometimes do, but when they observed that Helen was acting out very dramatic and realistic scenes, they became concerned. Dr. Flournoy at first put them at rest, insisting that she was merely expressing a theme that was the product of her subliminal self.

Later, when she entered a sanitorium he changed his mind. It became clear that the young woman was re-enacting scenes from a very distant past and that in her somnabulism she was repeating experiences that might easily be an earlier incarnation; or that spirits from a bygone age were crowding into her normal ego.

Entering into the middle of the drawing room of the home, Helen came forward with eyes strained and hands outstretched. With considerable artistry she expressed a predicament which implied a forthcoming ordeal, walking several times around an imaginary object with reverential gestures. As if clairvoyant, Dr. Flournoy saw into her movements a ritual being performed. "I believe it is a funeral pyre," he whispered. "She will soon throw herself onto the flames in an act of devotion to her dead husband."

Sure enough, Helen walked slowly round and round the imaginary pit of fire. Her countenance had assumed a deathly pale appearance. After finishing these circuits, she stooped and washed her hands in what was meant to be a running stream. Then she stood erect and solemnly addressed someone who must have been her son: "Take this poniard which your father employed over his enemies. Never use it for any other purpose. Govern your subjects wisely, as he did."

She then threw rice from what was supposed to be a plate in her hand. This was later found to be a custom of suttee to bring happiness to those who were able to catch any grains. Disrobing herself, first of her nonexistent tiara, then upper colored silks, which she handed to the unseen crowd of onlookers, she turned towards the flaming pyre, pronounced the names of her gods. Uttering piercing groans, she forthwith threw herself onto it and swooned until the sacrifice was consummated.

Helen did not remember any of her somnabulism. A striking fact about further nocturnal performances was that they appeared to follow the inverted order of historical chronology. This, Professor Flournoy soon recognized was quite in keeping with the theory that memories of a past existence revert first to the more recent occurrences and later to the more remote. On this basis it became possible to piece together the story of Helen's previous Hindu existence, or, if one prefers, of the earthly life of the spirit invading these somnabulistic trances. As her acting unrolled the story, it seemed she was once the daughter of a wealthy Arab shiek, living at the close of the Fourteenth Century. At about eighteen she had become the wife of a Hindu potentate.

As Princess Samandini she was passionately devoted to her

husband Raja Nayaka, who reigned over the fortress Tchandraguiri. He died in 1401 and she elected to become a suttee, that is she wanted to be burned alive at his funeral so she could enter Nirvana with him.

The number of women who became suttees was so large in India, Flournoy doubted that he could trace any record of Princess Samandini. In fact all the Hindu names Helen had recited could not be checked on. The tenacious psychologist, however, persisted until he found a confirmation. In an ancient tome by a long unread author named De Marles, a copy of which he located at the British Museum, he came across the following: "Kamara and neighboring provinces on the side towards Delhi may be regarded as the Georgia of Hindustan ... Tchandrauguiri, which signifies Mountain of the Moon, is a vast fortress constructed by the Raja Nayaka, who died in 1401."

Unfortunately, this discovery did not cure Helen Smith of her neuroticism and she died in the sanitorium on Lake Leman, aged 32, of natural causes.

A MESSAGE OF CONSPIRACY

In the halcyon days between the world wars, the 8th Marquess of Londonderry and his wife used to divide their time between their palatial estate, Mount Stewart, in Northern Ireland, and their town home in Park Lane, London. Lady Londonderry was a handsome, spirited woman who refused to abandon her childhood nickname of Circe. Like the Grecian daughter of Helios, she was certainly an enchantress and surrounded herself with the celebrities of her times—such as Ramsay MacDonald, whom she adored in spite of his red politics. Another was Field Marshal Sir Henry Wilson, a gifted Irishman whose name will live forever in the annals of the British Army.

In June 1922, Circe had these two lions staying at Mount Stewart. MacDonald was soon to become Prime Minister and Sir Henry had just been elected a Member of Parliament for

North Down. His maiden parliamentary speech was marked by such brilliant oratory that his political future seemed assured. The two men were poles apart politically, but they were personal friends. Everyone was set for a pleasant weekend. There were the usual country pursuits of shooting, hunting, and fishing.

On the night before Sir Henry and Lady Wilson were scheduled to leave for important appointments in London, Circe awoke from a terrible nightmare, crying loudly to her husband: "Sir Henry has been murdered. He was shot at close quarters. Someone must tell Lady Wilson."

Lord Londonderry soon calmed her, assuring her that Sir Henry was safe and sound in the west wing, which was almost impregnable to outsiders. This was verified next morning at breakfast when he never seemed healthier or happier. Circe told him about her dream and narrated the details minutely. She saw two short men firing revolvers at him from close range and, strangest of all, she noticed Sir Henry trying to defend himself with a sword which he was wearing as an appendage to full-dress military attire. The great Irish soldier was used to any situation and had been under fire several times at the front of battle, so he just laughed it off. He added that if it ever happened he hoped he would have a better defense than the sword, which he had never used. Circe's dream was ridiculed by all present, including Ramsay MacDonald. He said that would never be possible to happen if he became Prime Minister!

On June 22, only ten days after the dream, the Field Marshal officiated in full-dress uniform at the unveiling of the War Memorial at Liverpool Street Station in London. Returning alone to his home by taxi he alighted at the entrance of 36 Eaton Place. Two Irish hired assassins advanced towards him and fired at point blank. Their first shot missed and Sir Henry drew his sword, rushing at them. But a second volley sent him sprawling on the pavement, bleeding profusely and mortally wounded.

Naturally Lady Londonderry was obsessed by her nocturnal premonition, which she records in her autobiography

Retrospect. An interesting fact deduced from evidence at the trial of the murderers, who were later hanged, was that the plot to kill Wilson was at the precise time of her dream.

LINES TO LIVE BY

The national newspaper supplement, *This Week* Magazine, once asked me to make some submissions for the series, *Words to Live By,* in which authors expanded their thoughts on famous lines that had stimulated them intuitively. The one of mine accepted was bought also for the book rights, so I cannot reproduce it here. However, I feel the following rejections are better than the one accepted (writers soon learn that they only propose and editors dispose!), and so I publish them for the first time now because they seem to fit into the theme of my book.

* * * * * * * * *

> That you were born a certain day on earth
> All things and forces tended for that birth.
>
> Sir William Watson

Maybe you feel you ought to have become a starring performer, a ruling politician, or some other headliner? Instead you have been forced to sit on the sidelines and watch others of less ability go to the top. Actually, you should be congratulating yourself on being born at exactly the right time and place. You came here as a pilgrim soul to achieve a personality and to accomplish what no other person could. You were born into a very personal situation which began before you were born and will continue after you die. No one else can handle it but you. In case you don't realize it, a number of people would gladly change places with you, although they would never tell you. And those whom you envy are possibly recriminating about their personal status more than yourself!

* * * * * * * * *

The mind is its own place and in itself
Can make a Heaven of a Hell, and a Hell of Heaven.

John Milton

With the appalling number of Americans today seeking
psychiatric therapy, these words are especially significant. We
are all apt to fear the worst, but as soon as our minds can
estimate the full extent of any damage, the crisis is really
more than half over. Milton was stressing the mental law of
balance, which is similar to the one underlying the Universe.
In his own blindness he saw more beautiful visions than do
those with eyes to see; just as Beethoven heard in his deafness
more heavenly music than our more sensitive ears can ever
hear. Milton was saying that if the mental horizon is clear,
the outer world can be a place of ineffable loveliness.

* * * * * * * * *

So I dream until I come across a Cavalry
Set upon a solitary hillock.

John Addington Symons

Read any autobiography and you will come across a Cavalry.
Like everyone else, the writers had their unguarded hour
when the soul was tested almost beyond endurance. We all
come to this hour, some sooner than later, when seemingly
we face utter failure. It is then that all our past experience—
both good and bad—emerges from our subconscious mind,
where it has been "programmed" to extricate us. The Cavalry
can be conquered. Failure can only be permanent if you let it
keep you down.

* * * * * * * * *

I am now strengthened to understand things
differently and to admit that I have often blun-
dered.

Soren Kierkegaard

This entry in the diary of the man who also wrote "I am a
lonely wanderer in the hands of God," refers to the human
pettiness which causes estrangements and misunderstandings
between friends and makes enemies. Unfortunately, we all

are apt to call our blunders mistakes instead of the other way round. If both sides of any misunderstanding were willing to admit their error, they would still be bound by indissoluble ties. The world would be much nearer to the Golden Age, but the rarest soul in the world is he who is willing to admit being in the wrong.

* * * * * * * *

Oh! Say there is dawning another new day
Now, will you let it pass useless away?
Thomas Carlyle

I have seen many more dawns than most because I rise at that hour nearly every day. The dawn speaks, in its grimly beautiful way, of a coming expanse out of which good or bad can transpire. This same mysterious whitening light was seen through the crevices of caves inhabited by Neanderthalic man, telling him a new day was being born. Carlyle is explaining that difference. Today, each dawn is offering us a chance to spend an invisible currency, which is a measured time the cavemen did not know. Carlyle is saying that each hour is golden and is set with sixty diamond minutes.

As we age, we learn that there is more than one type of time, for our years go by like six months. This is because our sense of biologic time is aware we have much less left than when younger, so it speeds up our conscious chronology of events. It makes most of us much more far-sighted mentally, as well as ocularly—only two of many compensations. But just as most people give no thought of money until it is scarce, so they treat this invisible form of it. Killing time is like slowly committing suicide! The best way to save time is not to lose it.

* * * * * * * *

Let it be booked with the rest of this day's deeds.
William Shakespeare

For many years a London barrister I knew puzzled all of us by a mysterious little black book in which he scribbled entries now and then. It was not until he died that the mystery was explained. His Last Will was almost a replica of that little black book. It was found that every day he was plotting, intriguing, and discovering deserving cases that could use his beneficence. In his Will he insisted that every bequest be anonymous. In a larger sense our lives might be compared to a text book which can be read at the end of each day. No one else can fully understand it because it is written only as we could have done so. Each individual brain is an embrace of many spiritual minerals made up of many more cells than we can ever use. You alone can think the words to put into this book. Let it be filled with some wonderful spoils.

* * * * * * * * *

The strongest man in the world is the man who is most alone.

Henrik Ibsen

To learn to be alone is a difficult discipline for most Americans, who love activity. Hours passed alone should stand out like a mountain peak and should define the difference between being alone and loneliness. Without isolation there can be no inner life with which to oppose the disgraces of the outside world. I would say, however, that the strongest man in the world is he who can detach himself from all his materialistic wealth and look back upon it as a loan.

* * * * * * * * *

Most of our shadows are caused by standing in our own sunshine.

Ralph Waldo Emerson

If we understand the ramifications of the subconscious mind, we know we are actually part of a larger self—a far greater part than we have any way of knowing, where shadows form uncontrolled. Emerson is saying that we should look to the sunshine of others if we want to free our consciousness from

160

bondage. Even if most of us form a small part in the scheme of things, we can at least develop it well. Life will continue to give us successively sunshine and shadow, alternating as on an April day—but by standing aside in the shade, we will fix our attention on our own failings instead of others.

* * * * * * * * *

Under the fell clutch of circumstance
My head was bloody but unbowed.

W.E. Henley

The nearer to the physical extinction of a creative artist, the more passionately does he press on to create his best work. This is proven by poems written during a crisis of the poet's life, such as Mr. Henley was suffering when he wrote these famous lines. He is telling us that there is more to the human spirit than merely a triumph over adversity, that those who face devastating situations with an undefeated spirit make the world a richer place than before the blow struck. They make their personal tragedy an estimable gain for humanity at large. This enters the cosmos, where it will forever be reflected.

* * * * * * * * *

He taught us how to die.

Death of Addison by Thomas Tickell

Shortly before he was going to die, Thomas Addison called his wayward son to his bedside. "I wish," said he, "that you watch me now so you will know what it is to expire." Because of a long and blameless life the great essayist knew how to die. He knew that death is merely an experience that precedes the sunrise. He died serenely because he was convinced that his death was a carefully organized process for the fulfillment of a divine design. For him it was a call to the unchanging spiritual world of his ancestors. For us all it should be regarded as an appointed time to be postponed as long as possible.

* * * * * * * * *

161

The last great enemy to overcome is death.

Saint Paul

Without ever being able to experience any of the tremendous spiritual encounters of the great saint, I believe that he is suggesting, in his cryptic way, that if we understand the esoteric forces in our midst, we can keep death at bay in our thoughts. When he said: "I die daily," it seems to me he meant his mind must die a series of successive deaths so as to discard its imperfections. Our great privilege is to be present at these personal mutations, when we are given the opportunity to climb over our dead selves—seeing our new selves as from beyond the tomb. This is the shortest way to arrive at the center of spiritual gravitation.